Globalization

OPPOSING VIEWPOINTS®

Other Books of Related Interest

Opposing Viewpoints Series

The Environment
Epidemics
Global Resources
Global Warming
Pollution
Poverty
Technology and Society
Terrorism
War

Current Controversies Series

Developing Nations
Global Warming
War

At Issue Series

Are Efforts to Reduce Terrorism Successful?
Child Labor and Sweatshops
Does the World Hate the United States?
Do Infectious Diseases Pose a Serious Threat?
Is Global Warming a Threat?
How Can the Poor Be Helped?
Is the Gap Between the Rich and Poor Growing?

Globalization

OPPOSING VIEWPOINTS®

Louise I. Gerdes, *Book Editor*

Bruce Glassman, *Vice President*
Bonnie Szumski, *Publisher*
Helen Cothran, *Managing Editor*

GREENHAVEN PRESS
An imprint of Thomson Gale, a part of The Thomson Corporation

THOMSON
GALE

Detroit • New York • San Francisco • San Diego • New Haven, Conn.
Waterville, Maine • London • Munich

For more information, contact
Greenhaven Press
27500 Drake Rd.
Farmington Hills, MI 48331-3535
Or you can visit our Internet site at http://www.gale.com

LIBRARY OF CONGRESS CATALOGING-IN-PUBLICATION DATA

Globalization / Louise I. Gerdes, book editor.
p. cm. — (Opposing viewpoints series)
Includes bibliographical references and index.
ISBN 0-7377-2937-6 (lib. : alk. paper) — ISBN 0-7377-2938-4 (pbk. : alk. paper)
1. Globalization. I. Gerdes, Louise I., 1953– . II. Opposing viewpoints series (Unnumbered)
JZ1318.G57862 2006
303.48'2—dc22 2005040431

Printed in the United States of America

"Congress shall make no law. . . abridging the freedom of speech, or of the press."

First Amendment to the U.S. Constitution

The basic foundation of our democracy is the First Amendment guarantee of freedom of expression. The Opposing Viewpoints Series is dedicated to the concept of this basic freedom and the idea that it is more important to practice it than to enshrine it.

Contents

Chapter 3: How Does Globalization Affect Developing Nations?

Chapter 4: What Global Policies Are Best?

Why Consider Opposing Viewpoints?

"The only way in which a human being can make some approach to knowing the whole of a subject is by hearing what can be said about it by persons of every variety of opinion and studying all modes in which it can be looked at by every character of mind. No wise man ever acquired his wisdom in any mode but this."

John Stuart Mill

In our media-intensive culture it is not difficult to find differing opinions. Thousands of newspapers and magazines and dozens of radio and television talk shows resound with differing points of view. The difficulty lies in deciding which opinion to agree with and which "experts" seem the most credible. The more inundated we become with differing opinions and claims, the more essential it is to hone critical reading and thinking skills to evaluate these ideas. Opposing Viewpoints books address this problem directly by presenting stimulating debates that can be used to enhance and teach these skills. The varied opinions contained in each book examine many different aspects of a single issue. While examining these conveniently edited opposing views, readers can develop critical thinking skills such as the ability to compare and contrast authors' credibility, facts, argumentation styles, use of persuasive techniques, and other stylistic tools. In short, the Opposing Viewpoints Series is an ideal way to attain the higher-level thinking and reading skills so essential in a culture of diverse and contradictory opinions.

In addition to providing a tool for critical thinking, Opposing Viewpoints books challenge readers to question their own strongly held opinions and assumptions. Most people form their opinions on the basis of upbringing, peer pressure, and personal, cultural, or professional bias. By reading carefully balanced opposing views, readers must directly confront new ideas as well as the opinions of those with whom they disagree. This is not to simplistically argue that everyone who reads opposing views will—or should—change his or her opinion. Instead, the series enhances readers' understanding of their own views by encouraging confrontation with opposing ideas. Careful examination of others' views can lead to the readers' understanding of the logical inconsistencies in their own opinions, perspective on why they hold an opinion, and the consideration of the possibility that their opinion requires further evaluation.

Evaluating Other Opinions

To ensure that this type of examination occurs, Opposing Viewpoints books present all types of opinions. Prominent spokespeople on different sides of each issue as well as well-known professionals from many disciplines challenge the reader. An additional goal of the series is to provide a forum for other, less known, or even unpopular viewpoints. The opinion of an ordinary person who has had to make the decision to cut off life support from a terminally ill relative, for example, may be just as valuable and provide just as much insight as a medical ethicist's professional opinion. The editors have two additional purposes in including these less known views. One, the editors encourage readers to respect others' opinions—even when not enhanced by professional credibility. It is only by reading or listening to and objectively evaluating others' ideas that one can determine whether they are worthy of consideration. Two, the inclusion of such viewpoints encourages the important critical thinking skill of objectively evaluating an author's credentials and bias. This evaluation will illuminate an author's reasons for taking a particular stance on an issue and will aid in readers' evaluation of the author's ideas.

It is our hope that these books will give readers a deeper understanding of the issues debated and an appreciation of the complexity of even seemingly simple issues when good and honest people disagree. This awareness is particularly important in a democratic society such as ours in which people enter into public debate to determine the common good. Those with whom one disagrees should not be regarded as enemies but rather as people whose views deserve careful examination and may shed light on one's own.

Thomas Jefferson once said that "difference of opinion leads to inquiry, and inquiry to truth." Jefferson, a broadly educated man, argued that "if a nation expects to be ignorant and free . . . it expects what never was and never will be." As individuals and as a nation, it is imperative that we consider the opinions of others and examine them with skill and discernment. The Opposing Viewpoints Series is intended to help readers achieve this goal.

David L. Bender and Bruno Leone,
Founders

Greenhaven Press anthologies primarily consist of previously published material taken from a variety of sources, including periodicals, books, scholarly journals, newspapers, government documents, and position papers from private and public organizations. These original sources are often edited for length and to ensure their accessibility for a young adult audience. The anthology editors also change the original titles of these works in order to clearly present the main thesis of each viewpoint and to explicitly indicate the opinion presented in the viewpoint. These alterations are made in consideration of both the reading and comprehension levels of a young adult audience. Every effort is made to ensure that Greenhaven Press accurately reflects the original intent of the authors included in this anthology.

Introduction

"Much of the talk of 'globalization' is confused and confusing. 'Globalization' has become a buzzword—and those using the term often have contrasting understanding of what it means."

—Mark K. Smith, British writer and educator

The World Trade Organization (WTO), an organization of 148 nations that promotes unfettered global trade, held one of its periodic summits in Seattle, Washington, in November 1999. At that time most observers viewed open trade among the world's nations as a positive force; thus the WTO members gathered in Seattle anticipated what journalist Brian Hansen called "a festival of 'free trade.'" These hopes were dashed, however.

On November 30, fifty thousand protesters, who, among other concerns, believe WTO policies wreak havoc on the environment and threaten the lives of the world's poor, packed downtown Seattle. Although most protesters practiced nonviolent civil disobedience, some lit bonfires, smashed store windows, and threw debris at local police. To prepare for then-president Bill Clinton's arrival, federal officials ordered the Seattle police to clear the streets. The police, while moving block by block through the city, fired tear gas, robber bullets, and concussion grenades at anyone in their way. The city resembled a war zone as armored vehicles and helicopters patrolled the streets. In the end local businesses sustained $12.5 million in property damage. More than five hundred people were arrested, although most charges were later dropped. For activists, the protest was a success: WTO delegates did not reach a new trade agreement, and the antiglobalization movement reached center stage.

Many observers were unclear as to what exactly these activists were protesting. They were unsure what globalization was and why some people might be opposed to it. Shortly after the protests in Seattle, the word began to appear more frequently in the news. According to journalist Doug Henwood, "After flatlining its way through the 1980s and early '90s, 'globalization'—as a word, at least—took off in a near-vertical ascent in the late 1990s." Nevertheless, many remain unclear what globalization means. When thirty Americans in a focus group were asked what globalization meant to them, the respondents complained about the rapid pace of modern life, feelings of powerlessness, and growing gaps between haves and have-nots. Academic understanding is not much clearer. Jan Edward Garrett, professor of philosophy at Western Kentucky University in Bowling Green claims, "There is in fact a growing academic industry consisting of attempts to define 'globalization' and specify its significance." Several definitions of globalization have emerged. Two of the most common definitions—one equating globalization with internationalization, the other with modernization—provide a framework for the globalization debate.

Some commentators equate globalization with internationalization, the increasing economic integration and interdependence of countries. Supporters use this definition to bolster their claim that globalization improves life for open nations that embrace it and harms people in closed nations that do not. "The more closed the economy," claims Robert D. Hormats, vice chairman of Goldman Sachs International, a global investment banking and securities firm, "the greater the likelihood that very large numbers of citizens suffer from poverty and are deprived of access to the flow of communications, commerce, visitors and ideas that enhance human liberty and creativity."

Globalization's opponents contend that increasing economic interdependence is not always a beneficial force for the world's poor. Many opponents are not against globalization itself, but against, as Cambridge University economics professor Amartya Sen puts it, "the inequality in the overall balance of institutional arrangements—which produces very unequal sharing of the benefits of globalization." Critics argue that although globalization can provide developing nations with much-needed wealth, often that wealth has ended up in the pockets of those who already have the lion's share of it—shareholders and executives in large multinational corporations. Opponents also claim that tariffs and other policies that protect domestic interests are now mostly forbidden by WTO trade agreements and the institutions that lend money to developing nations, such as the International Monetary Fund (IMF) and the World Bank. However, developed nations such as the United States can implement protective trade policies that protect their domestic interests because they have the strength to override WTO agreements and do not need to borrow money from the IMF and World Bank. Poor nations do not have this power and so are at a disadvantage.

The second definition equates globalization with modernization. Advances in telecommunications technology that accelerate and expand access to media and the Internet expose more of the world to new opportunities, values, and products. Supporters argue that in addition to spreading medical and scientific advances, globalization will spread democratic ideals as people around the world become aware of the freedoms that people in the West enjoy. Because they will want the same things for themselves, supporters reason, people living under repressive regimes will force their governments to move toward democracy.

Globalization opponents claim, however, that exposure to Western ideology and technology does not necessarily foster democracy or improve human welfare. In fact, they contend, quite the opposite can be true. The institutions of globalization are, according to Sen, "much more concerned with expanding the domain of market relations than with, say, establishing democracy, expanding elementary education, or enhancing the social opportunities of society's underdogs." He adds, "International business concerns often have a strong preference for working in orderly and highly organized autocracies rather than in activist and less-regimented democracies, and this can be a regressive influence on equitable development."

Supporters and opponents continue to shape people's understanding of globalization. Their views are presented in the following chapters of *Opposing Viewpoints: Globalization:* How Does Globalization Affect Society? How Does Globalization Affect the Global Community? How Does Globalization Affect Developing Nations? What Global Policies Are Best? The way that people conceive of globalization can have important implications for the world in the years ahead. As international studies professor Jan Aart Scholte writes, "Knowledge is power, and intellectual constructions of globalization help to shape the course of the trend."

CHAPTER 1

How Does Globalization Affect Society?

Chapter Preface

International trade is the engine of globalization, spreading goods, capital, and information worldwide. Unfortunately, since groups of people first began trading with one another, trade has also contributed to the spread of disease. Most historians agree that trading ships bore the black rats that carried bubonic and pneumonic plague to Europe in 1347, for example. Modern international trade has not only increased the speed and efficiency of trade but the speed at which disease can spread. Syndicated columnist Ellen Goodman writes, "The world has shrunk to the size of an airplane ticket. And germs don't need a visa. You can have breakfast in Beijing, dinner in London and end up hospitalized in Toronto."

However, international trade has also led to the creation of international health organizations that have proved effective in combating global plagues. The expansion of travel and trade in the first half of the nineteenth century, for example, raised concerns in Europe and North America about the importation of diseases from Asia, Africa, and Latin America, which prompted the first international health initiatives. "Realizing that national strategies, such as quarantine, were useless without international cooperation," claims law professor David P. Fidler, "European governments launched a series of international sanitary conferences and treaties that spanned the second half of the nineteenth and the first half of the twentieth centuries." The international health movement also led to the establishment of the United Nations World Health Organization (WHO), which some claim was instrumental in stopping the spread of severe acute respiratory syndrome (SARS) in 2003.

The SARS epidemic is an example of just how quickly diseases can now spread. On February 11, 2003, the Chinese Ministry of Health sent a report to WHO describing an outbreak of an acute respiratory syndrome in the Guangdong Province of China. An infected medical doctor carried SARS out of Guangdong to the ninth floor of a hotel in Hong Kong. According to WHO, "Days later, guests and visitors to the hotel's ninth floor had seeded outbreaks of cases in the hospital systems of Hong Kong, Viet Nam, and Singapore.

Simultaneously, the disease began spreading around the world along international air travel routes as guests at the hotel flew home to Toronto and elsewhere." In the end SARS killed at least 774 people worldwide. The disease not only threatened global public health, it also inflicted heavy blows to the economies of Hong Kong, Singapore, Vietnam, and Toronto.

While globalization has facilitated the spread of diseases such as SARS, it also has aided efforts to combat infectious diseases. "If the disease went international with unprecedented speed, so did the response. If oceans no longer can keep people or germs on their own side of the water, nor can they keep researchers apart," Goodman contends. Once advised of the SARS outbreak, WHO researchers in thirteen labs in ten countries put all other work aside and within weeks identified the coronavirus as the cause of SARS. They also developed a diagnostic test. Analysts worldwide claim that WHO was instrumental in helping detect and isolate those infected, slowing the spread of the disease.

For some commentators the SARS epidemic serves as a wake-up call about the dangers of globalization. Professor Fidler contends, "Today, developed countries—like the aristocratic courtiers in Edgar Allan Poe's 'Masque of the Red Death' who believed that crenellated castle walls would protect them from the pestilence without—are belatedly realizing the cost of their complacency about infectious diseases." Other analysts see globalization in more positive terms. "Before the cough heard round the world becomes a symbol of local vulnerability, let it also be said that the way the world has mobilized against [SARS] is an equal and opposite sign of the value of our connections," Goodman claims. Commentators continue to debate the impact of globalization on public health. The authors in the following chapter explore other controversies in the debate over globalization's impact on society.

VIEWPOINT 1

"Globalization represents a giant qualitative leap forward in the history of humankind."

Globalization Is Beneficial to Society

Abbas J. Ali

Abbas J. Ali claims in the following viewpoint that the global expansion of trade creates beneficial interdependence among nations. Because geography is no longer a barrier to cooperation, he contends, nations have joined together to fight common enemies such as AIDS, poverty, and terrorism. Moreover, true globalization respects diverse cultures, allowing less-powerful nations to benefit from free trade without having to conform to more powerful nations' values. Ali, a business professor at Indiana University of Pennsylvania, is executive director of the American Society for Competitiveness, which promotes unrestricted international trade.

As you read, consider the following questions:

1. According to Ali, why might it be dangerous for globalization to become an intellectual "play zone"?
2. How does the author define *connectivity*?
3. How has the relationship between benefits and responsibilities changed from previous world systems, in the author's opinion?

Abbas J. Ali, "In Defense of Globalization," *Competitiveness Review*, vol. 11, Winter/Spring 2001, p. 1.

The debate about and the use of the term "globalization" is in a state of flux. In the business world, globalization has become the fashionable term for CEOs to use in presentations and in their annual reports. In academia, the globalization concept has attracted the attention of both eminent and emerging scholars and has become a focal point for serious research and theory development. Furthermore, the intense focus of the media on "globalization" has made it a part of both "popular culture" and world consciousness.

A Term Subject to Bias

The growing interest in the concept of globalization among scholars, policy makers, and business people, however, increases the probability that the term will be used in contradictory ways and more importantly that it will be misused in the service of the dominant forces in a given society. This may induce bias in the discourse on globalization, thereby rendering it into the service of special interest groups instead of the entire global community. [Jacques] Attali (1997) warns that on the global scale there are powerful minorities that seek to take full advantage of the market economy. These groups want total control of world resources and come to view the democratic participation of poor majorities as intolerable burdens. Attali's concern is well founded. In certain quarters in the world, there are many voices that do not shy away from claiming monopoly over globalization benefits. These forces consider globalization not as a collective journey but as exclusive privileges for the elites or the dominant superpower, the U.S. For example, [Benjamin] Cohen (1998), [David] Rothkopf (1997), and [Kenneth] Waltz (2000), among others, view globalization as domination or homogenization. This conceptualization lacks morality and is certainly a threat to world stability.

In the academic literature, [Roland] Robertson (1992) cautions that there is a danger that globalization "will become an intellectual 'play zone,' a site for the expression of residual social theoretical interests, interpretive indulgence, or the display of world ideological preferences." This could spread confusion and doubt relative to the process and aims. For example, in the management literature, globalization is treated as internationalization, trade or market expansion or the production and distribution of goods and services of a similar type and quality on a worldwide basis. The major drawback of these views is deeper than simplicity of the definition. Rather, these views eventually tend to empty globalization from its true meaning and intent, thereby deepening doubt about globalization.

Globalization symbolizes commitment and desire for a better future. It conveys optimism, and offers infinite possibilities for growth, renewal, and revitalization for every participant in world society. That is, globalization represents a giant qualitative leap forward in the history of humankind. Its underlying assumptions revolve around shared responsibilities and benefits. In the business world globalization conveys interdependence, integration, and connectivity of the world community. Based on this and familiarity with the latest conceptual developments in the areas of global and competition studies, the following definition of globalization is suggested: globalization is a set of beliefs that fosters a sense of connectivity, interdependence, and integration in the world community. It highlights commonalties without overlooking differences, and it extends benefits and responsibilities on a global scale. In terms of business operations, globalization means the ability of a corporation to conduct business across borders in an open market, and the maximizing of organizational benefits, without inflicting social damage or violating the rights of people from other cultures.

Interdependence, Connectivity, and Integration

There are certain elements in the above definition that are important for understanding the linkage between business operations and societal development:

Interdependence. This refers to the fact that in the globalization era, events that take place in a given country have an immediate and direct impact on other countries. For example, in March 2001, many countries had to build emergency defenses against the spread of foot-and-mouth disease that threatens the livestock in various continents. Countries and societies no longer live and operate as isolated self-sustained entities. In addition, these events influence the business operations and market position of corporations. For example, Procter & Gamble on February 26, 2001, cited the economic crisis in Turkey and the devaluation of its currency, the lira, as the reason for the possible decline in its profits.

Connectivity. This is a qualitative aspect of the human journey across time. People are aware, regardless of their geographical space, of the existence of a world community. Connectivity refers to the fact that today's communities, groups and individuals across the globe share a common set of expectations and principles. That is, these forces across the globe anticipate civility in behavior and conduct. In fact, civility becomes the foundation for global transformation. Likewise, connectivity means that geography and times are no longer a major constraint for people to interact, participate, and be involved in activities globally. Information technology, openness and corporate activities render many of the psychological and physical barriers obsolete.

The Globalization of Human Well-Being

During the last half century, as wealth and technological change advanced worldwide, so did the well-being of the vast majority of the world's population. Today's average person lives longer and is healthier, more educated, less hungry, and less likely to have children in the workforce. Moreover, gaps in these critical measures of well-being between the rich countries and the middle- or low-income groups have generally shrunk dramatically since the mid-1900s irrespective of trends in income inequality. However, where those gaps have shrunk the least or even expanded recently, the problem is not too much globalization but too little.

Indur M. Goklany, *Policy Analysis*, August 22, 2002.

Integration. Minimizing the impact of negative events and maximizing benefits become more than ever a collective endeavor. Fighting AIDS, corruption, money laundering, drugs, poverty, economic crises, and environmental and terrorist threats, for example, is no longer confined to one government. Governments all over the world along with non-government organizations and corporations have to join resources together to design programs and strategies to eliminate or reduce threats to the well-being of the world community. World economic and trade activities clearly accelerate interdependence and integration. At this time, these activities have been accompanied by cultural and political transformations that have profoundly altered world realities and intensified connectivity.

Awareness of Commonalities and Dissimilarities. This is one of the most misunderstood elements. Some think-tank intellectuals suggest that the globalized world must be created according to the image of the existing superpower(s). That is, there must be a global unification of cultural, economic, and to some degree political orientations. Globalization, however, neither seeks unification nor promotes convergence. Indeed, globalization, in its spirit and aims, appreciates differences and treats them as a foundation for human self-expression, creativity, and co-existence. Globalization provides a fine balance between pragmatism and idealism. Thereby, it lays the foundation for civility and for genuine tolerance and diversity. It is worth mentioning, however, that convergence around effective organizational practices and in areas of trade rules and regulations, and human rights is more likely to take place.

Advancing Diversity

Global corporations and executives advance diversity and consider differences, be they ethnical or otherwise, as a foundation for open markets and competition. Global corporations, therefore, do not support or promote global cultural and economic unification. They understand that the world's diversity in all its forms manifest opportunities and dynamism. For example, [multinational corporation] Caterpillar (1992) asserts,

> It isn't our aim to remake the world in the image of any one country or philosophy. Rather, we hope to help improve the quality of life, wherever we do business, by serving as a means of transmission and application of knowledge that has been found useful elsewhere. We intend to learn and benefit from human diversity.

Similarly, Cor Herkstroter (1996), Chairman of the Dutch/Shell Group, argues that "[t]hose who would impose one standard on the whole globe, the moral imperialists are clearly wrong." Global managers, unlike politicians, are not comfortable with hegemony. William Holland (1996), Chairman and CEO of United Dominion Industries, asserts that businesspeople should "question the so-called 'facts' that politicians and media send out." He calls for nurturing understanding among citizens of the world rather than dominating others. This signifies a fundamental difference between hegemonic and global managers' orientations toward global affairs. Global managers perceive globalization as an inclusive process that maximizes participation and induces access to global economic and technological benefits.

Shared Benefits and Responsibilities. Previous world systems condoned benefits for the hegemonic power and giant corporations but released them from any moral or economic obligation to the rest of the world. In the globalization era, benefits and responsibilities go hand in hand. Not only in an open market system do goods and services cross borders with minimum or no barriers but also rules of law are observed. Furthermore, corporations view the whole globe as the arena for their activities. No market or region is ignored or left behind. Corporations pursue opportunities in every corner of the world and simultaneously consider the present and potential consequences of their activities on the communities and regions where they operate. All global actors' activities are scrutinized and transparency is normal.

The preceding elements highlight the nature of globalization as a concept that will enable the world community to step forward with optimism about the ability to overcome formidable obstacles. It profoundly alters the world realities and offers the business community and the public at large the reason to flourish. Most importantly, however, globalization sustains the collective journey of humankind and sets the stage for a more prosperous and democratic world.

VIEWPOINT 2

"Globalization threatens earth's life systems, undermines cultural integrity and diversity, and endangers the lives of many who are poor."

Globalization Is Harmful to Society

Cynthia Moe-Lobeda

In the following viewpoint Cynthia Moe-Lobeda argues that the central mechanisms of globalization are destructive. For example, economic growth is not always good: Expansion that leads to higher profits for corporations may harm the environment by destroying resources, she maintains. Moreover, Moe-Lobeda asserts, market freedom does not inevitably lead to political freedom but in fact threatens liberty. For example, the free market now allows corporations to patent seeds, forcing poor farmers to purchase seeds from these companies at high prices, threatening the farmers' economic livelihoods. Moe-Lobeda, professor of technology and social ethics at Seattle University School of Theology, is author of *Healing a Broken World: Globalization and God.*

As you read, consider the following questions:

1. In Moe-Lobeda's opinion, why does society acquiesce to the prevailing form of globalization?
2. According to the author, what does growth theory fail to recognize about the earth?
3. What hybrid form of "homo economicus" has emerged in the United States in the last few decades, in the author's view?

The pathos of the situation stuns. Christians are called, before all else except love for God, to love neighbor as self. This is our gift and vocation, our primary lifework here on earth, and many of us long to fulfill it. Yet we find ourselves locked into a global political economy that structures exploitation into the very fabric of our lives. We do not wish to buy shirts made in sweatshops, coffee grown on land that should feed its hungry children, or metal products from mines that have displaced thousands of people. We are not pleased to be pumping toxins into our planetary home, destroying the life systems upon which life depends. Yet, we do.

A Spiritual Crisis

Our lives are intimately bound up in a moral-spiritual crisis of profound and unprecedented dimensions. The reigning model of economic globalization threatens earth's life systems, undermines cultural integrity and diversity, and endangers the lives of many who are poor in order that some might consume exorbitantly and a few accumulate vast wealth. According to the 1998 United Nations Human Development Report, globalization "is concentrating power and marginalizing the poor, both countries and people. . . . The world's 225 richest people have a combined wealth of over $1 trillion, equal to the annual income of the poorest 47 percent of the world's people."

A haunting dimension of that crisis is our acquiescence to the prevailing form of globalization. As a society, we do not seriously consider its long-term social and ecological implications. We fail to resist it and forge alternatives. Many of us, insulated by privilege, remain blind to the suffering and ecological devastation wrought by current global trade and investment regimes. Others, while aware, feel muted, dwarfed by the situation, and powerless to shape economic lifestyles and structures that enhance human and planetary flourishing. . . .

Globalization is not simply a set of laws, regulations, and economic and political arrangements. It is built upon several very specific ideological presuppositions—what I call "market myths." Uncritically accepted, these market myths form a comprehensive view of human life, freedom, laws of nature and society, and historical inevitability. Together, they serve as a bulwark against envisioning alternative economic arrangements. The ideology underlying globalization functions, in effect, as a kind of gospel: a proclamation of saving truth, and of how we are to live in the world. Our first challenge is to name and scrutinize these myths, unmask the false gospel. As Jesus urges, we must see.

Not All Growth Is Good

The first "market myth" undergirding economic globalization is that growth benefits all. At the heart of globalization is the movement to deregulate (or "liberalize") trade and investment from all constraints. That movement is supported by the presupposition that "free" or "open" markets lead to economic growth, which benefits all. Proponents of globalization push for deregulation and liberalization of foreign trade and investment, in order to generate economic growth which, they claim, will result in increased prosperity, employment, and living standards for most people.

Without a doubt, liberalization generates economic growth, which has reaped incredible bounty for a good many and has enabled many others to escape poverty. Deception lies in the claim that growth necessarily translates to greater economic well-being for all. This presupposition is invalid for a number of reasons.

First, the Gross Domestic Product or GDP measurement (which tracks growth in a nation's economy by tallying the amount of services and goods produced and paid for) fails to account for the social and ecological costs of growth. GDP does not distinguish between destructive and sustaining economic activity. All economic activity is measured as positive. An excessively consumptive lifestyle is considered a moral "good" because it generates growth, regardless of the trash and toxins spawned. Indicators of breakdown in families, communities, and health can also count as growth: Ten-year-olds purchasing cigarettes, alcoholics feeding their addiction, and the sale of pornography all contribute to growth.

The Flaws in Growth Theory

The GDP treats the extraction of natural resources as income rather than as the depletion of an asset. When a forest is cut down in the mountains of the Philippines, destroying sustenance for indigenous peoples, the deforestation registers as growth. GDP measurement fails to account for the costs borne by the larger society and future generations as a result of a business transaction. Water pollution, disease, injury due to workplace hazards, and toxic waste—none of these are factored as costs when growth figures are calculated.

A Rising Tide Does Not Lift All Boats

Corporate globalization was promoted as something that would (eventually) benefit all the people of the world. It would help reduce poverty, create more jobs, and even benefit the environment. "A rising economic tide will lift all boats," we were assured [by former president Bill Clinton]. . . .

Far from lifting all boats, economic globalization has lifted only the yachts. And this obscene inequity has become transparently obvious to people all over the world. They now see the devastating effects of neoliberalism on their livelihood, their social programs, their culture, their environment and their sovereignty.

Ed Finn, *Catholic New Times*, September 7, 2003.

Growth theory also fails to take into account distribution of wealth and income. For instance, economists point to a 22.2 percent growth in average household worth in the United States from 1983 to 1998. Yet the number of homeless people increased, more and more people were unable to obtain healthcare, and many citizens experienced severe economic insecurity and job loss. The growth indicators don't spell out that the wealthiest one percent experienced skyrocketing increases in income, while middle- and lower-income families saw their incomes shrink. So while the average household wealth increased, the median household net worth decreased by 10 percent in the same period.

In addition, the claim that continued growth will benefit all fails to recognize the earth's natural limits. Free-market theory assumes that growth has no fixed limits, and that boundless economic expansion will bring all people to a state of prosperity as defined by Western middle-class standards. Yet, as many economists, scientists, environmentalists, and ethicists now point out, the human economy is part of a much larger planetary economy of life. That economy's limits in both renewable and nonrenewable resources have been so pushed that unchecked growth now further destroys earth's regenerative capacity.

Finally, growth as measured by GDP is an inadequate and inaccurate measure of economic well-being because GDP attributes to a host country corporate profits which actually are returned to the company's home country. So when a U.S.-based corporation makes a profit at its plant in Guatemala and returns much of that profit to the United States, it still registers as growth for Guatemala.

Yes, globalization promotes growth. However, the claim that growth benefits all is exposed as false when we ask the crucial questions: Growth for whom? And growth at what cost?

Differing Conceptions of Freedom

A second myth at the heart of global free-market ideology is that human freedom and market freedom are inseparably linked. According to this claim, human freedom is grounded in private property and the freedom to do with one's property as one pleases in the marketplace.

Politically, market freedom is seen as a necessary condition for democratic freedom. Advocates of globalization contend that expanding government, especially through taxation and regulation, threatens basic human liberties, because it constrains people's freedom to use possessions as they choose. They argue that people are free to use the earth's resources for the sake of profit—a freedom that extends to those persons who can buy access to those resources.

Freedom, thus understood, is for doing as one pleases with one's money and other property, and is freedom from the demands of the widespread good and from public accountability, scrutiny, regulation, and responsibility. Market freedom takes on supreme and universal value. Other values are sacrificed to it. Labeling economic and financial activity as "free"—the terminology of inalienable moral rights—associates it with freedom of the human spirit, political freedom, moral freedom, and democracy.

This essential market myth, too, is fraught with deception.

Globalization's version of freedom clashes with the reality of countless human beings whose freedom to survive is threatened by free trade and investment. One very telling example: The World Trade Organization agreement on Trade-Related Intellectual Property (TRIPS) grants global corporations the right to patent seeds developed over generations by indigenous farmers. Under TRIPS agreements, subsistence farmers in India and other nations—whose ancestors developed the seed strains—may no longer save that patented seed from one year to the next but must instead pay an annual fee to use it. Basmati rice, an important Indian export, was patented by the Texas-based company Rice-Tec after it slightly altered the Indian rice. Indian farmers no longer may export the rice without paying Rice-Tec for the right to do so. (Another attempted use of TRIPS is to create seeds that will geminate only when used with agrochemicals sold by the particular company that owns the seed.) To advocates of TRIPS, this is "market freedom." To many others, it is "biopiracy" that threatens their economic livelihood. . . .

Whenever "freedom" or "free" is attached to market activity, we must ask the revealing questions ignored in the mad stampede of globalization: Freedom from what, for whom, toward what end, and with what public accountability? The freedom lauded by global free-market proponents has served to concentrate wealth, pauperize millions, and jeopardize the earth's regenerative capacity, while distracting us from alternative notions of freedom that could nurture sustainable and just socio-ecological communities. Our task is to reclaim and reconstruct "non-market" notions of freedom, such as freedom to flourish as whole beings-in-community and freedom to use one's gifts not only toward the well-being of self and loved ones but also toward the well-being of human communities and the larger community of life.

Homo Economicus

A third key myth in the prevailing paradigm of economic globalization holds that the human being is, above all, an economic being—homo economicus. That is, human beings are essentially autonomous rational subjects rather than beings-in-community, competitive rather than cooperative, and consumeristic rather than spiritual. In economic life, people are motivated almost entirely by self-interest measured by personal financial gain, and have the inalienable and divinely ordained right to pursue that self-interest. Individual autonomy is expressed most fully through acquisition and protection of private property. Those who own and consume the most are the most valued human beings.

In the last few decades, at least in the United States, homo economicus has assumed a hybrid form: homo consumens. Human beings are essentially consumers. Economic growth, the goal of globalization, requires ever-increasing consumption. George W. Bush blessed this hybrid by declaring an annual "national day of the consumer."

Many economists now argue that the driving force of advanced capitalism is not production but consumption. The expansion of world consumption in the past century is staggering—but it has been accompanied by vast disparities. The money spent annually on pet food in North America and Europe would more than pay for basic education and installation of water and sanitation for all who now go without, worldwide. The amount spent annually on perfume by North Americans and Europeans would nearly cover basic healthcare and adequate nutrition for all who lack. Biblical theologian Walter Brueggemann writes, "Consumerism is not simply a market strategy. It has become a demonic spiritual force among us."

A related dimension of homo economicus is homo dominans. Rooted in Christian theologies of human dominion over nature, homo dominans assumes that the earth exists for human use, and that, by divine mandate, the human species has dominion over the rest of creation. Although theologies of domination have been challenged eloquently by recent feminist, eco-feminist, and earth-honoring theologies, dominion theologies still prevail in the world-view underlying the globalizing economy.

The Commodification of Human Life

The definition of humans as homo economicus, consumens, and dominans constitutes the operative moral anthropology at the heart of economic globalization. Human worth is placed in relationship to buying power. Descendants of the tribes of Europe—and especially males among them—control vastly more of the earth's wealth and resources than people of color. As a result, they are viewed as inherently more valuable and more fully human, and are afforded more human rights, including the right to make decisions regarding the shape of economic and cultural life for all people.

Since people are defined by their economic transactions, and some people have only their bodies to sell (for labor or for sex), some human beings are commodities. Their bodies are to be purchased at the lowest price the market will bear. A pre-NAFTA [North American Free Trade Agreement] advertisement encouraging corporations to locate plants in Mexico and Central America featured Rosa Galvez, who could be hired for fifty-four cents an hour. A year after NAFTA was enacted, the same ad featured Rosa at thirty-seven cents an hour.

Such a vision of human personhood is dangerously dehumanizing and destructive, both for human communities and for the earth. A task before us is to lift up a different vision of the human person, in the context of human community and of earth-community, and imbued with inherent worth—in other words, the heart of a biblical vision.

The False Science

Finally, free-market ideology includes the myth that corporate- and-finance-driven globalization is inevitable. It is evolutionary, a contemporary form of Manifest Destiny, a step in modernity's march of progress. The emerging structures of global political economy are historically unavoidable. Societies must adjust to it or face the consequences.

This presupposition is grounded in a Western view of economics as a positivist science, in line with irrefutable, objective principles, much as Newtonian physics. The economic laws rationalizing globalization are presumed to be universal, value-free structures of reality, rather than morally laden human constructs. Economic theories operate detached from and oblivious to actual historical contexts. Some economists have even argued, in line with homo economicus, that the laws governing market economics are reflective of all human life and practice. Rational self-interest, it is argued, is no less than a way of life, applicable to all human behavior.

Ironically, Adam Smith, the father of free-market theory, was not in synch with such a universalization of free market as "way of life." Smith distrusted the morality of the market as a morality for society at large. Smith neither envisioned nor prescribed a capitalist society, but rather a capitalist economy within a society guided by noncapitalist and nonmarket morality—including, according to Smith, mutual neighborly love; an obligation to practice justice; a norm of financial support for the government "in proportion to [one's] revenue;" and a tendency in human nature to derive pleasure from the good fortune and happiness of other people.

The assumed inevitability of globalization is perhaps the most powerful myth. If globalization is inevitable and natural, no legitimate and viable alternatives exist. Of course, this dynamic is as old as history: A power structure absolutizes itself and its authority by claiming it belongs to the proper order of the cosmos.

Yet, another dynamic is also centuries old: There are always people who refuse the myth, who open their eyes and see clearly that a given power structure is not natural, universal, or inevitable, but is instead the product of human decisions and designs. Like the many "inevitable" power systems before it, economic globalization can be resisted, subverted, or changed—but only when we begin to unmask the powerful illusions that seduce us into acquiescence with it. Instead, we must recover a vision of who we are called and empowered by God to be: human beings-in-community-of-life, crafting ways of living that enable the household of earth to flourish, and all people to have the basic material, cultural, and political necessities for life with dignity.

"Globalization not only increases individual freedom, but also revitalizes cultures and cultural artifacts."

Globalization Benefits the World's Cultures

Philippe Legrain

Globalization does not impose cultural uniformity but creates greater cultural freedom, claims Philippe Legrain in the following viewpoint. The Americanization of world cultures is a myth, he argues; many American cultural exports take on the cultural flavor of the nations that import them. Moreover, he contends, cross-cultural exchange spreads diversity, strengthening all cultures. Those who want to preserve cultural purity impose their cultural preferences on others who desire the freedom to enjoy the foods, traditions, and languages of many nations. Legrain is an economist and the author of *Open World: The Truth About Globalization.*

As you read, consider the following questions:

1. According to Legrain, what is the beauty of globalization?
2. In what areas is America not a global leader, in the author's view?
3. In the author's opinion, what Western ideas are taking root almost everywhere?

Philippe Legrain, "In Defense of Globalization: Why Cultural Exchange Is Still an Overwhelming Force for Good," *International Economy*, vol. 17, Summer 2003, p. 62.

Fears that globalization is imposing a deadening cultural uniformity are as ubiquitous as Coca-Cola, McDonald's, and Mickey Mouse. Many people dread that local cultures and national identities are dissolving into a crass all-American consumerism. That cultural imperialism is said to impose American values as well as products, promote the commercial at the expense of the authentic, and substitute shallow gratification for deeper satisfaction.

Thomas Friedman, columnist for the *New York Times* and author of *The Lexus and the Olive Tree*, believes that globalization is "globalizing American culture and American cultural icons." Naomi Klein, a Canadian journalist and author of *No Logo*, argues that "Despite the embrace of polyethnic imagery, market-driven globalization doesn't want diversity; quite the opposite. Its enemies are national habits, local brands, and distinctive regional tastes."

But it is a myth that globalization involves the imposition of Americanized uniformity, rather than an explosion of cultural exchange. And although—as with any change—it can have downsides, this cross-fertilization is overwhelmingly a force for good.

The Freedom to Choose

The beauty of globalization is that it can free people from the tyranny of geography. Just because someone was born in France does not mean they can only aspire to speak French, eat French food, read French books, and so on. That we are increasingly free to choose our cultural experiences enriches our lives immeasurably. We could not always enjoy the best the world has to offer.

Globalization not only increases individual freedom, but also revitalizes cultures and cultural artifacts through foreign influences, technologies, and markets. Many of the best things come from cultures mixing: Paul Gauguin painting in Polynesia, the African rhythms in rock 'n' roll, the great British curry. Admire the many-colored faces of France's World Cup–winning soccer team, the ferment of ideas that came from Eastern Europe's Jewish diaspora, and the cosmopolitan cities of London and New York.

Fears about an Americanized uniformity are overblown.

For a start, many "American" products are not as all-American as they seem; MTV in Asia promotes Thai pop stars and plays rock music sung in Mandarin. Nor are American products all-conquering. Coke accounts for less than two of the 64 fluid ounces that the typical person drinks a day. France imported a mere $620 million in food from the United States in 2000, while exporting to America three times that. Worldwide, pizzas are more popular than burgers and Chinese restaurants sprout up everywhere.

In fashion, the ne plus ultra is Italian or French. Nike shoes are given a run for their money by Germany's Adidas, Britain's Reebok, and Italy's Fila. American pop stars do not have the stage to themselves. According to the IFPI [International Federation of the Phonographic Industry], the record-industry bible, local acts accounted for 68 percent of music sales in 2000, up from 58 percent in 1991. And although nearly three-quarters of television drama exported worldwide comes from the United States, most countries' favorite shows are homegrown.

Nor are Americans the only players in the global media industry. Of the seven market leaders, one is German, one French, and one Japanese. What they distribute comes from all quarters: Germany's Bertelsmann publishes books by American writers; America's News Corporation broadcasts Asian news; Japan's Sony sells Brazilian music.

In some ways, America is an outlier, not a global leader. Baseball and American football have not traveled well; most prefer soccer. Most of the world has adopted the (French) metric system; America persists with antiquated British Imperial measurements. Most developed countries have become intensely secular, but many Americans burn with fundamentalist fervor—like Muslims in the Middle East.

Examining Hollywood Domination

Admittedly, Hollywood dominates the global movie market and swamps local products in most countries. American fare accounts for more than half the market in Japan and nearly two-thirds in Europe. Yet Hollywood is less American than it seems. Top actors and directors are often from outside America. Some studios are foreign-owned. To some extent,

Hollywood is a global industry that just happens to be in America. Rather than exporting Americana, it serves up pap to appeal to a global audience.

Hollywood's dominance is in part due to economics: Movies cost a lot to make and so need a big audience to be profitable; Hollywood has used America's huge and relatively uniform domestic market as a platform to expand overseas. So there could be a case for stuffing subsidies into a rival European film industry, just as Airbus was created to challenge Boeing's near-monopoly. But France's subsidies have created a vicious circle whereby European film producers fail in global markets because they serve domestic demand and the wishes of politicians and cinematic bureaucrats.

The Impact on Language

Another American export is also conquering the globe: English. By 2050, it is reckoned, half the world will be more or less proficient in it. A common global language would certainly be a big plus—for businessmen, scientists, and tourists—but a single one seems far less desirable. Language is often at the heart of national culture, yet English may usurp other languages not because it is what people prefer to speak, but because, like Microsoft software, there are compelling advantages to using it if everyone else does.

But although many languages are becoming extinct, English is rarely to blame. People are learning English as well as—not instead of—their native tongue, and often many more languages besides. Where local languages are dying, it is typically national rivals that are stamping them out. So although, within the United States, English is displacing American Indian tongues, it is not doing away with Swahili or Norwegian.

Even though American consumer culture is widespread, its significance is often exaggerated. You can choose to drink Coke and eat at McDonald's without becoming American in any meaningful sense. One newspaper photo of Taliban fighters in Afghanistan showed them toting Kalashnikovs—as well as a sports bag with Nike's trademark swoosh. People's culture—in the sense of their shared ideas, beliefs, knowledge, inherited traditions, and art—may scarcely be eroded by mere commercial artifacts that, despite all the furious branding, embody at best flimsy values.

The really profound cultural changes have little to do with Coca-Cola. Western ideas about liberalism and science are taking root almost everywhere, while Europe and North America are becoming multicultural societies through immigration, mainly from developing countries. Technology is reshaping culture: Just think of the Internet. Individual choice is fragmenting the imposed uniformity of national cultures. New hybrid cultures are emerging, and regional ones reemerging. National identity is not disappearing, but the bonds of nationality are loosening.

Cross-Cultural Exchange

Cross-border cultural exchange increases diversity within societies—but at the expense of making them more alike. People everywhere have more choice, but they often choose similar things. That worries cultural pessimists, even though the right to choose to be the same is an essential part of freedom.

Cross-cultural exchange can spread greater diversity as well as greater similarity: more gourmet restaurants as well as more McDonald's outlets. And just as a big city can support a wider spread of restaurants than a small town, so a global market for cultural products allows a wider range of artists to thrive. If all the new customers are ignorant, a wider market may drive down the quality of cultural products: Think of tourist souvenirs. But as long as some customers are well informed (or have "good taste"), a general "dumbing down" is unlikely. Hobbyists, fans, artistic pride, and professional critics also help maintain (and raise) standards.

A bigger worry is that greater individual freedom may undermine national identity. The French fret that by individually choosing to watch Hollywood films they might unwittingly lose their collective Frenchness. Yet such fears are overdone. Natural cultures are much stronger than people seem to think. They can embrace some foreign influences and resist others. Foreign influences can rapidly become domesticated, changing national culture, but not destroying it. Clearly, though, there is a limit to how many foreign influences a culture can absorb before being swamped. Traditional cultures in the developing world that have until now evolved (or failed to evolve) in isolation may be particularly vulnerable.

The Contradiction of Cultural Pessimism

In *The Silent Takeover*, Noreena Hertz describes the supposed spiritual Eden that was the isolated kingdom of Bhutan in the Himalayas as being defiled by such awful imports as basketball and Spice Girls T-shirts. But is that such a bad thing? It is odd, to put it mildly, that many on the left support multiculturalism in the West but advocate cultural purity in the developing world—an attitude they would tar as fascist if proposed for the United States. Hertz appears to want people outside the industrialized West preserved in unchanging but supposedly pure poverty. Yet the Westerners who want this supposed paradise preserved in aspic rarely feel like settling there. Nor do most people in developing countries want to lead an "authentic" unspoiled life of isolated poverty.

An Optimistic Perspective

I wish to offer [an] . . . optimistic perspective on global culture. My vision of globalized culture looks to Hong Kong cinema, the novels of Garcia Marquez, the Cuban music of Buena Vista Social Club, the successes of Australian Aboriginal art, and the amazing proliferation of ethnic dining. Culture lovers have never had more quality choices than today, and artists have never had more opportunities to reach audiences. Insofar as we have a "global shopping mall," it delivers many diverse styles to eager fans around the world.

Tyler Cowen, *Phi Kappa Phi Forum*, Fall 2003.

In truth, cultural pessimists are typically not attached to diversity per se but to designated manifestations of diversity, determined by their preferences. Cultural pessimists want to freeze things as they were. But if diversity at any point in time is desirable, why isn't diversity across time? Certainly, it is often a shame if ancient cultural traditions are lost. We should do our best to preserve them and keep them alive where possible. Foreigners can often help, by providing the new customers and technologies that have enabled reggae music, Haitian art, and Persian carpet making, for instance, to thrive and reach new markets. But people cannot be made to live in a museum. We in the West are forever casting off old customs when we feel they are no longer relevant. Nobody argues that Americans should ban nightclubs to force people back to line dancing. People in poor countries have a right to change, too.

Moreover, some losses of diversity are a good thing. Who laments that the world is now almost universally rid of slavery? More generally, Western ideas are reshaping the way people everywhere view themselves and the world. Like nationalism and socialism before it, liberalism is a European philosophy that has swept the world. Even people who resist liberal ideas, in the name of religion (Islamic and Christian fundamentalists), group identity (communitarians), authoritarianism (advocates of "Asian values") or tradition (cultural conservatives), now define themselves partly by their opposition to them.

Faith in science and technology is even more widespread. Even those who hate the West make use of its technologies. Osama bin Laden plots terrorism on a cellphone and crashes planes into skyscrapers. Antiglobalization protesters organize by e-mail and over the Internet. China no longer turns its nose up at Western technology: It tries to beat the West at its own game.

A Two-Way Street

Yet globalization is not a one-way street. Although Europe's former colonial powers have left their stamp on much of the world, the recent flow of migration has been in the opposite direction. There are Algerian suburbs in Paris, but not French ones in Algiers. Whereas Muslims are a growing minority in Europe, Christians are a disappearing one in the Middle East.

Foreigners are changing America even as they adopt its ways. A million or so immigrants arrive each year, most of them Latino or Asian. Since 1990, the number of foreign-born American residents has risen by 6 million to just over 25 million, the biggest immigration wave since the turn of the 20th century. English may be all-conquering outside

America, but in some parts of the United States, it is now second to Spanish.

The upshot is that national cultures are fragmenting into a kaleidoscope of different ones. New hybrid cultures are emerging. In "Amexica" people speak Spanglish. Regional cultures are reviving. The Scots and Welsh break with British monoculture. Estonia is reborn from the Soviet Union. Voices that were silent dare to speak again.

Individuals are forming new communities, linked by shared interests and passions, that cut across national borders. Friendships with foreigners met on holiday. Scientists sharing ideas over the Internet. Environmentalists campaigning together using e-mail. Greater individualism does not spell the end of community. The new communities are simply chosen rather than coerced, unlike the older ones that communitarians hark back to.

Creating New Identities

So is national identity dead? Hardly. People who speak the same language, were born and live near each other, face similar problems, have a common experience, and vote in the same elections still have plenty in common. For all our awareness of the world as a single place, we are not citizens of the world but citizens of a state. But if people now wear the bonds of nationality more loosely, is that such a bad thing? People may lament the passing of old ways. Indeed, many of the worries about globalization echo age-old fears about decline, a lost golden age, and so on. But by and large, people choose the new ways because they are more relevant to their current needs and offer new opportunities.

The truth is that we increasingly define ourselves rather than let others define us. Being British or American does not define who you are: It is part of who you are. You can like foreign things and still have strong bonds to your fellow citizens. As Mario Vargas Llosa, the Peruvian author, has written: "Seeking to impose a cultural identity on a people is equivalent to locking them in a prison and denying them the most precious of liberties—that of choosing what, how, and who they want to be."

VIEWPOINT

"Global cultural homogenization is sweeping the world."

Globalization Harms the World's Cultures

Maude Barlow

In the following viewpoint Maude Barlow contends that globalization imposes American culture on other nations. For example, American movies dominate the world film market, she claims, and local filmmakers are finding that Hollywood film formulas are trumping local innovation. Many American corporations, with the support of the World Trade Organization, impose trade rules that make it difficult for local cultural producers to compete against them. To prevent the homogenization of the world's cultures, international agreements must be drawn up that protect local cultures, she argues. Maude Barlow is chair of the Council of Canadians, an organization that advances alternatives to corporate-style free trade.

As you read, consider the following questions:

1. In Barlow's view, what percentage of the world's languages may no longer be spoken by the end of the twenty-first century?
2. According to the author, what message is being sent to cultural sectors that do not totally pay their own way?
3. In the author's opinion, how can the balance between the free flow of art and cultural diversity be maintained?

Maude Barlow, "The Global Monoculture: 'Free Trade' Versus Culture and Democracy," *Earth Island Journal*, Autumn 2001.

Global cultural homogenization is sweeping the world. Indian physicist and activist Vandana Shiva calls it "monoculture of the mind." Dominated by US and Western values and lifestyles, driven by a consumer-based, free-market ideology and carried through the massive US entertainment-industrial complex, the global monoculture has infiltrated every corner of the Earth.

In China, Latin America, the Pacific Region, South America, Africa and the industrialized world, young people want Nike sneakers, Gap clothes, [basketball star] Michael Jordan T-shirts, the latest CDs, Hollywood blockbuster movies, American television and mass-market books. Around the world, North American corporate culture is destroying local tradition, knowledge, skills, artisans and values.

The Decline of Artisanship

Artisans groups trying to sell their products locally have been wiped out by global fashions. Much more than an economic problem, the decline of artisanship may be consuming some of the world's older traditions and finer crafts and eroding the world's cultural diversity, with little notice.

There are no clear estimates of the number of artisans in the world, although some crafts groups believe it is the largest employer outside agriculture. Says the *Toronto Globe and Mail*'s John Stackhouse, "With each endangered craft are centuries of songs, expressions and lifestyles that are part of an artisan's creative environment." Nawal Hassan, an Egyptian artisan-activist, adds, "This is an issue of identity. All our civilization has ceased to be spiritual. Our civilization has become commercial."

Combined with the destruction of the habitat of aboriginal citizens in many parts of the world, this assault on local cultures is having a profound impact. Hundreds of languages spoken today are lost each decade and it is estimated that one-half of the world's 6,000 languages will no longer be spoken or read by the end of the 21st century.

Technology is also advancing one culture and one language. The US has more computers than the rest of the world combined. English is used in 80 percent of websites, yet fewer than one in ten people worldwide speak the language. Everywhere, Internet access divides educated from illiterate, rich from poor, young from old and urban from rural. For many countries feeling the deadening and harmonizing impacts of economic globalization, protecting cultural diversity has become as important a fight as preserving biodiversity.

Many societies, particularly indigenous peoples, view culture as their richest heritage, without which they have no roots, history or soul. Its value is other than monetary. To commodify it is to destroy it.

There is a growing sentiment in many parts of the world that culture is not just another product like steel or computer parts. Through funding programs, content regulations and other public policies, countries have encouraged their own artists and cultures and tried to maintain some space for their own intellectual creations.

Culture as Business

The entertainment-industrial complex, on the other hand, sees culture as a business—a very big business that should be fiercely advanced through international trade agreements like the World Trade Organization (WTO). This industry combines giant telecommunications companies, cable companies and the Internet, working together in a complex web. The productions issuing from this superweb include publishing, films, broadcasting, video, television, cable and satellite systems, mega-theater productions, music recording and distribution, and theme parks.

Mass-produced products of popular culture are the biggest US export, according to the United Nations 1999 Human Development Report. A huge, well-organized coalition links the US entertainment, media and information technology sectors in a "common front" to oppose cultural protectionism. Companies such as AOL Time-Warner and Disney have powerful friends on Capitol Hill and in the White House. They work closely with the government, which in turn has taken a very aggressive stand in protecting their interests.

The pending admission of China into the WTO[1] has the

1. China was admitted to the WTO on December 11, 2001.

US motion picture industry salivating. Already, the 10 US films allowed in every year totally dominate the Chinese market. Zhang Hui Jun of the prestigious Beijing Film Academy fears that the US invasion will induce Chinese producers to slavishly follow Hollywood's formulas at the expense of innovative Chinese productions.

For many years, the US State Department has used a variety of trade remedies to strike down nation, state and local rules aimed at protecting indigenous cultures. In recent years, the battle has heated up as more countries adopt measures to support their own artists and cultural producers.

While it is true that these fights have shaped up more over film and TV than the live performing arts, the pressure to cut back on government funding for any cultural sector that does not totally pay its own way is growing in all countries. The messages are loud and clear: "Get big or die," and "Get a corporate sponsor or fold."

Canadians live next door to the world's biggest candy store. While we still have a vibrant, live performing arts community, government funding has been severely cut. Local theater productions have a hard time competing against imported US mega-productions and many theater halls across the country have been renamed for corporations that now sponsor the shows they fancy.

Culture and the WTO

Current WTO trade law subjects culture to all the disciplines of the agreement. There have been seven complaints concerning culture lodged at the WTO since its inception. Of those resolved, all effectively limited the right of a state to protect its cultural industries.

The most significant was a 1997 ruling in which the US successfully forced Canada to abandon protections for its magazine industry (even though US magazines make up 85 percent of all magazines available on Canadian newsstands). The US is taking a hard line because any exemption for Canada will set a precedent for other countries, especially in the developing world where cultural protection is just emerging as an issue.

Former US Trade Representative Charlene Barshefsky

triumphantly declared that the decision would serve as a useful weapon against other countries' attempts to protect their film, books and broadcasting industries.

The US State Department remains furious about the role that Canadian cultural activists played in defeating the Multilateral Agreement on Investment (MAI)[2] several years ago.

The "Theme-Parking" of Culture

The "theme-parking" of culture, which is part of globalization and part of the theme-parking of our world is, yes, a kind of diversity, but it is the diversity of the theme park. It is increasingly synthetic; it's increasingly distanced from the authentic origin. Increasingly, it takes a toll on that authentic origin, as when an American crêpe maker ends up back in Paris selling the American version of crêpes to people in Paris who don't make them anymore because there's a much cheaper global product they can get in place of what they've had. Globalization has a tendency to move that process forward at alarmingly dispiriting rates.

Benjamin Barber, *CATO Policy Report*, May/June 2003.

According to Christopher Sands of the Washington-based Center for Strategic and International Studies, "What further startled US policymakers was to hear these Canadian arguments echoed in Europe and even Asia. In an increasingly small world, ideas travel fast, and the Canadian concern that the MAI would lead to greater American cultural hegemony touched a chord around the world." The lesson for US trade negotiators was clear: "Canada's example matters."

The failure of the 1999 WTO talks in Seattle doesn't mean the problems for the cultural community are over. Ongoing talks related to the General Agreement on Trade in Services (GATS) and Trade-Related Intellectual Property rights (TRIPS) have placed the entire telecommunications sector—including the Internet, broadcasting, patents, trademarks and copyright law—on the table.

Speaking before a House committee in early 2000, Barshefsky vowed to use the WTO to promote US corporate-

2. MAI would have liberalized rules for international investment, thus promoting globalization.

entertainment interests around the world. "We are developing proposals for a wide range of sectors where our companies have strong commercial interests," she said. "Our companies are poised to be among the primary beneficiaries from stronger commitments at the WTO."

Toward Cultural Diversity

Trade is as old as humanity. Fair trade rules can be a positive development if done with respect for other aspects of life. But in recent years, the WTO has overtaken every other sphere of life, enforcing free trade rules on behalf of powerful transnational corporations. This, in turn, profoundly affects every culture in the world, basically enforcing a for-profit model on every aspect of society and denigrating any activity that is not, at its core, commercial.

What can be done? How can we maintain the free flow of intellectual creations and art, while promoting diversity in the face of a giant, centralized, monolithic corporate/cultural juggernaut backed by international trade regimes?

The debate is about finding ways to provide choice, so that in the deluge of cultural products available, citizens can choose to watch, listen to, or enjoy a book, magazine, film or sound recording that reflects their own local reality. More than anything else, the debate is about cultural diversity.

I have four strong recommendations. First, our governments must fund a vibrant cultural sector in all of our countries, one that reflects the diverse, local and indigenous societies in which they, and we, thrive.

Second, culture must be carved out of free trade agreements, particularly the WTO. Although citizens and their governments are still very likely to want to promote the export of their cultural products, they must always retain the right to set fair-trade conditions in order to protect and promote their own stories, history and unique culture.

Third, it is time for a new international instrument to deal with this emerging issue. To succeed, such an instrument must have a status equivalent to that of trade agreements. It cannot be subservient. It must recognize the importance of maintaining cultural diversity and set out rules that, over time, can be changed, since we cannot know today what form cultural expression may take in the future.

Finally, artists, writers, filmmakers and musicians from around the world must form an international civil society force to stand up to the corporate colossus now dominating global culture.

This process already has begun. [In 2002], a global network of nongovernmental organizations concerned about cultural issues met in Santorini, Greece, to form the International Network for Cultural Diversity. More than 160 organizations from more than 30 countries have committed themselves to becoming a powerful voice in the coming decades.

"As trade and globalization have spread . . . so too have democracy and political and civil freedoms."

Globalization Promotes Democracy

Daniel T. Griswold

Studies support the conclusion that a powerful correlation exists between globalization and democracy, maintains Daniel T. Griswold in the following viewpoint. According to Griswold, free trade fosters a sharing of ideas, exposes the world's people to the benefits of democracy, and enriches nations' citizens, who can then use that wealth as leverage to effect political change. Research bears out this hypothesis: Nations open to trade have been significantly more likely to extend political and civil freedom to their citizens. Griswold is director of the Cato Institute Center for Trade Policy Studies.

As you read, consider the following questions:

1. According to Griswold, how does a larger middle class help promote democracy?
2. By what percentage has the share of the world's population that enjoys full civil and political liberties grown from 1973 to today, according to Freedom House?
3. In the author's opinion, why do a few outliers not disprove the assertion that trade promotes democracy?

Daniel T. Griswold, "Trading Tyranny for Freedom: How Open Markets Till the Soil for Democracy," *Trade Policy Analysis*, January 6, 2004, pp. 2–6, 9–10.

Economic openness and the commercial competition and contact it brings can directly and indirectly promote civil and political freedoms within countries. Trade can influence the political system directly by increasing the contact a nation's citizens experience with the rest of the world, through face-to-face meetings, and electronic communications, including telephone, fax, and the Internet. Commercial communication can bring a sharing of ideas and exposure to new ways of thinking, doing business, and organizing civil society. Along with the flow of consumer and industrial goods often come books, magazines, and other media with political and social content. Foreign investment and services trade create opportunities for foreign travel and study, allowing citizens to experience first-hand the civil liberties and more representative political institutions of other nations.

Creating a Civil Society

Economic freedom and trade provide a counterweight to governmental power. A free market diffuses economic decisionmaking among millions of producers and consumers rather than leaving it in the hands of a few centralized government actors who could, and often do, use that power to suppress or marginalize political opposition. Milton Friedman, the Nobel-prize-winning economist, noted the connection between economic and political freedom in his 1962 book, *Capitalism and Freedom:*

> Viewed as a means to the end of political freedom, economic arrangements are important because of their effect on the concentration or dispersion of power. The kind of economic organization that provides economic freedom directly, namely competitive capitalism, also promotes political freedom because it separates economic power from political power and in this way enables the one to offset the other.

This dispersion of economic control, in turn, creates space for nongovernmental organizations and private-sector alternatives to political leadership—in short, civil society. A thriving private economy creates sources of funding for nonstate institutions, which in turn can provide ideas, influence, and leadership outside the existing government. A more pluralistic social and political culture greatly enhances the prospects for a more pluralistic and representative political system. Private-sector corporations, both domestic and foreign-owned, create an alternate source of wealth, influence, and leadership. Theologian and social thinker Michael Novak identified this as the "Wedge Theory," in which capitalist practices "bring contact with the ideas and practices of the free societies, generate the economic growth that gives political confidence to a rising middle class, and raise up successful business leaders who come to represent a political alternative to military or party leaders. In short, capitalist firms wedge a democratic camel's nose under the authoritarian tent."

The Advantages of Economic Freedom

Just as important, economic freedom and openness encourage democracy indirectly by raising living standards and expanding the middle class. Economic theory and evidence lean heavily toward the conclusion that open economies tend to grow faster and achieve higher incomes than closed economies. The *Economic Freedom of the World* study by James Gwartney and Robert Lawson found that nations that ranked in the top quintile in terms of economic openness from 1980 to 1998 experienced annual economic growth that was almost five times faster (2.4 percent vs. 0.5 percent) than those nations in the bottom quintile of openness. People living in the most open economies enjoyed far higher annual incomes per capita ($22,306 vs. $2,916) than those living in the most closed economies. A study by World Bank economists David Dollar and Aart Kraay found that less developed countries that opened themselves to the global economy grew much faster than those that remained relatively closed. Other academic studies have reached similar conclusions.

The faster growth and greater wealth that accompany trade promote democracy by creating an economically independent and politically aware middle class. A sizeable or dominant middle class means that more citizens can afford to be educated and take an interest in public affairs. As citizens acquire assets and establish businesses and careers in the private sector, they prefer the continuity and evolutionary reform of a democratic system to the sharp turns and occasional revolutions of more authoritarian systems. People who are allowed to successfully manage their daily economic lives in a relatively free market come to expect and demand more freedom in the political and social realms.

Cultivating Democracy

Economic development raises expectations that change and progress are possible. In less developed countries, it often leads to growing urbanization, which fosters greater literacy, communication, and access to alternative media. Palpable material progress can take the steam out of radical political movements that feed on frustration and hopelessness, and increase tolerance for minority ethnic and political groups. Ruling elites tend to treat their middle-class countrymen with more respect and deference than they would those in the impoverished and uneducated lower classes.

Political scientists have long noted the connection between economic growth, political reform, and democracy. As Seymour Martin Lipset observed in his classic study, *Political Man: The Social Bases of Politics:*

> The more well-to-do a nation, the greater the chances that it will sustain democracy. From Aristotle down to the present, men have argued that only in a wealthy society in which relatively few citizens lived at the level of real poverty could there be a situation in which the mass of the population intelligently participate in politics and develop the self-restraint necessary to avoid succumbing to the appeals of irresponsible demagogues.

Wealth by itself does not promote democracy if the wealth is controlled by the state or a small ruling elite. A resource-rich country can have a relatively high per capita gross domestic product, but if its natural wealth is centrally held and does not nurture an autonomous middle class that earns its wealth independently of the state, the prospects for political pluralism, civil liberties, and democracy are probably no better than in a poor country without resources. For wealth to cultivate the soil for democracy, it must be produced, retained, and controlled by a broad base of society, and for wealth to be created in that manner, an economy must be relatively open and free.

The reality of the world today broadly reflects those theoretical links between trade, free markets, and political and civil freedom. As trade and globalization have spread to more and more countries in the last 30 years, so too have democracy and political and civil freedoms. In particular, people who live in countries that are relatively open to trade are much more likely to live in democracies and enjoy full civil and political freedoms than those who live in countries relatively closed to trade. Nations that have followed a path of trade reform in recent decades by progressively opening themselves to the global economy are significantly more likely to have expanded their citizens' political and civil freedoms.

Twin Trends of Global Freedom

The recent trend toward globalization has been accompanied by a trend toward greater political and civil liberty around the world. In the past 30 years, cross-border flows of trade, investment, and currency have increased dramatically, and far faster than output itself. Trade barriers have fallen unilaterally and through multilateral and regional trade agreements in Latin America; the former Soviet bloc nations; East Asia, including China; and more developed nations as well.

During that same period, political and civil liberties have been spreading around the world. Thirty years ago democracies were the exception in Latin America, while today they are the rule. Many former communist states from the old Soviet Union and its empire have successfully transformed themselves into functioning democracies that protect basic civil and political freedoms. In East Asia, democracy and respect for human rights have replaced authoritarian rule in South Korea, Taiwan, Thailand, the Philippines, and Indonesia.

According to Freedom House, a New York–based human rights organization, the share of the world's population that enjoys full civil and political liberties has risen sharply in the past three decades. The share of the world's people who live in countries Freedom House classifies as "Free"—meaning "countries in which there is broad scope for open political competition, a climate of respect for civil liberties, significant independent civic life, and independent media"—has jumped from 35 percent in 1973 to 44 percent today. Meanwhile, the share of people living in countries classified as

"Not Free"—"where basic political rights are absent and basic civil liberties were widely and systematically denied"—has dropped from 47 to 35 percent. The share of people living in countries classified as "Partly Free"—those "in which there is limited respect for political rights and civil liberties"—has increased slightly from 18 to 21 percent.

The Expansion of Political and Civil Freedom, 1973 to 2003

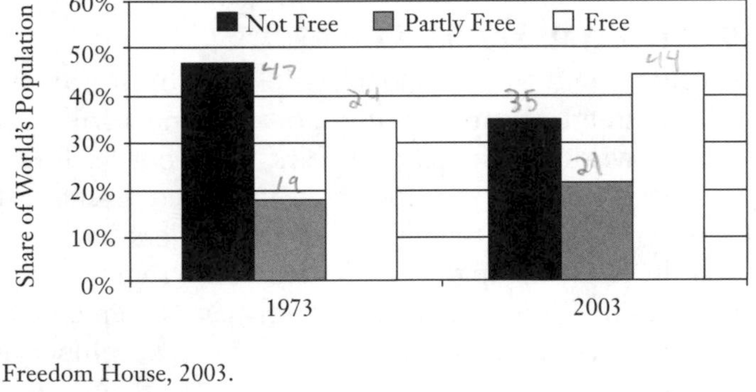

Freedom House, 2003.

As globalization accelerated in the late 1980s after the fall of the Berlin Wall, so too did the global trend toward democracy. Again, according to Freedom House, the share of the world's governments that are democratically elected has spiked from 40 percent in the mid-1980s to 63 percent in 2002–03. . . .

Economic Openness and Political and Civil Liberties

Behind the aggregate trends toward freedom is the question of whether those countries that have opened themselves to trade correlate with those that enjoy political and civil liberties today.

To measure the correlation between openness to trade and civil and political freedom among individual countries, this study uses two comprehensive and newly updated databases to compare economic and political/civil freedom in the world among a broad cross-section of countries. To measure political and civil freedom, we use Freedom House's annual *Freedom in the World* ratings. Freedom House rates virtually all of the world's nations and territories according to their political rights and civil liberties. The organization defines political rights as the ability of a nation's citizens "to participate freely in the political process. This includes the right to vote and compete for public office and to elect representatives who have a decisive vote on public policies." Civil liberties, according to the organization, "include the freedom to develop opinions, institutions, and personal autonomy without interference from the state."

To measure economic freedom and, more specifically, freedom to engage in international commerce, we use the Fraser Institute study, *Economic Freedom of the World*, which measures economic freedom in 123 countries. The study's authors, James Gwartney and Robert Lawson, measure economic freedom in five general areas: size of government; legal structure and security of property rights; access to sound money; regulation of credit, labor, and business; and freedom to exchange with foreigners. The last category will be used in this study to measure a nation's openness to trade and other forms of international commerce. The category includes taxes on international trade and nontariff regulatory trade barriers, the size of the trade sector, official versus black-market exchange rates, and restrictions on capital markets. Those countries rated by both databases encompass more than 90 percent of the world's population.

Comparing the two indexes reveals that nations with open and free economies are far more likely to enjoy full political and civil liberties than those with closed and state-dominated economies. . . .

Recognizing Outliers

Although economic and political freedoms tend to correlate across countries, the freedom to trade and engage in other economic activity does not always accompany civil and political freedom, nor does the absence of the one necessarily preclude the other. . . . Certain countries remain "outliers," defying the general trend. For example, Singapore trails only Hong Kong as the freest and most open economy in the world, yet it is rated only "Partly Free" in terms of political and civil liberties. At the opposite corner, India remains among the least open economies (despite recent reforms) and yet is a stable democracy, rated among the "Free" nations. Yet even in those two well-known exceptions, the underlying forces that connect political and civil freedom seem to be at work. Since 1991, India has moved decisively if incompletely away from its four-decade experiment in self-imposed economic isolation. Meanwhile, the government of Singapore faces growing pressure to relax its political and social restrictions in an effort to attract and retain more educated, middle-class professionals. Those same forces have been more visibly at work in Hong Kong, another economically open but "Partly Free" Southeast Asian city state where a prosperous and educated middle class have demanded full protection of their civil liberties and a more direct role in choosing their chief executive and representatives.

A few outliers do not disprove a powerful underlying correlation. Because of historical, cultural, and other factors, it would be unrealistic to expect nations to conform to the average correlation in strict linear fashion. Consider a parallel with smoking and human health. For decades, medical researchers have documented the statistical correlation between heavy smoking, lung cancer, and early death. Yet some heavy smokers live to a ripe old age, and nonsmokers can die prematurely from various causes. Those outliers do not disprove the correlation between smoking and diminished health and longevity. Similarly, an economy closed to international trade and commerce does not rule out a healthy body politic, just as an open economy does not guarantee one—but nations that pursue the latter economic policy are unmistakably healthier on average in their respect for political and civil freedoms.

By multiple means of measurement, political and civil freedoms do correlate in the real world with expanding freedom to trade and transact across international borders. Nations that have opened themselves over time to trade and foreign investment are indeed more likely to have opened themselves to political competition and thus expanded the freedom of their citizens to speak, assemble, and worship freely. Nations open today to international commerce are far more likely to be free from political and civil repression than those nations that remain closed. And around the globe, the broad expansion of international trade and investment has accompanied an equally broad expansion of democracy and the political and civil freedoms it is supposed to protect.

"At best a long-term ally in promoting democracy, [globalization] provides no automatic solutions."

Globalization Does Not Always Promote Democracy

Catharin E. Dalpino

Globalization does not ensure that authoritarian regimes will liberalize, argues Catharin E. Dalpino in the following viewpoint. Globalization increases the number of democracies in areas where democratic nations already dominate, but when a region is dominated by authoritarian regimes, global trade does not tend to promote the liberalization of nondemocratic states, she contends. Globalization can strengthen authoritarian regimes when it results in improved living conditions—citizens living in these nations attribute such advancements to their totalitarian governments, leading to greater support for them. Dalpino, a fellow at the Brookings Foreign Policy Studies program, is author of *Deferring Democracy: Promoting Openness in Authoritarian Regimes.*

As you read, consider the following questions:

1. In Dalpino's view, why is it not yet possible to make a final judgment about the connection between globalization and democracy?
2. According to the author, what are the limits of international norms of democracy?
3. Why is technology's impact on democratization not sufficient in itself to effect political change, in the author's opinion?

Catharin E. Dalpino, "Does Globalization Promote Democracy?" *Brookings Review*, vol. 19, Fall 2001, p. 45.

An enduring tenet of the post–Cold War era is that globalization is a catalyst for democratization. In one formulation when democratic ideals sweep (or even trickle) across borders into authoritarian states, globalization makes democratization inevitable. Proponents of this view point to the contagion of democratic transition in the world over the past quarter-century and to the ability of technology to penetrate the most closed societies. Even the Orwellian North Korean government,[1] they point out, has gone gingerly online, though the country's broader population has no electronic access to the outside world.

But these broad trends cannot yet confirm a strong and direct connection between globalization and democratization. The evidence is mixed and will continue to be so for some time. For every society in which a "people's power" revolution is helped along by international cheering squads and satellite television, another is daily becoming more cosmopolitan while adhering to traditional (and often authoritarian) practices. The city-state of Singapore, rated as "most global" on the A.T. Kearny/*Foreign Policy* magazine Globalization Index in terms of cross-border contact between people, has remained resolutely semi-authoritarian for the past 30 years and shows few signs of greater democratization. Moreover, while entire regions, particularly in the former Eastern bloc, embraced economic globalization and more open political processes at the onset of the 1990s, by the end of the decade many new democracies were faltering under the weight of globalization, whether because of unfavorable economic trends or greater transnational crime. It may not yet be possible to make a final judgment about the connection between globalization and democracy, but a closer look will clarify where globalization has helped democratization, where it has inhibited movement toward greater openness, and, assuming an increased pace of globalization, what the greater flows of people and ideas will mean for the world's governments and societies in the years ahead.

Perhaps the most tangible evidence of globalization's im-

1. An Orwellian government is totalitarian, evocative of the futuristic totalitarian state portrayed in the satirical novel *1984*, written by George Orwell.

pact on democratization has been the infusion of democratic norms, and the principles of human rights that support them, into many international and regional institutions. The principle of accountability for human rights abuse is increasingly unfettered by national borders, as the 1998 arrest of former Chilean President Augusto Pinochet [who is an alleged war criminal] in London demonstrated. The ad hoc United Nations war crimes tribunal that was convened for the former Yugoslavia in the early 1990s was extended to Rwanda in the middle of the decade, presaging a broader move toward international justice. . . . The establishment of an International Criminal Court will be a watershed in that move.

Democratic principles are also reshaping regional institutions. The European Union, originally an economic community, now requires democratic government as a precondition for membership and promotes democracy in its collective foreign policy. The Organization of American States, once a diplomatic forum for both democratic and nondemocratic governments, now works actively to restore democracy when it is imperiled in member states. The Organization of African Unity, also a traditional diplomatic group, is attempting to forge a regional human rights code modeled after the Helsinki process in Europe.

The Limits of International Norms

But the process has its limits. Regional groups adopt codes of democratic practice where a quorum of democracies already exists or where the largest and most economically powerful states are democratic. In these cases, the weight of the democratic majority (and the benefits of membership in the club) are sometimes sufficient to help persuade nondemocratic states to liberalize. But the trend halts abruptly where the political spectrum includes an equal number of democratic and nondemocratic states or where authoritarian regimes are predominant. In Asia, for example, the diversity of political regimes has largely kept democracy and human rights off the table in the Asian-Pacific Economic Cooperation (APEC) group and the Association of Southeast Asian Nations (ASEAN).

A more encouraging but more low-level trend has been

the growth of transnational nongovernmental organizations [NGOs] devoted to promoting democracy and protecting human rights. These groups, which usually originate and are headquartered in Western nations, establish beachheads (and nurture local counterparts) in authoritarian nations, although they are seldom able to operate there without significant restrictions. Thus, in regions where authoritarian trends remain strong—most notably in Asia and the Middle East—the only networks dedicated to spreading democratic values and strengthening human rights are nongovernmental. For the foreseeable future, the best chance of building intergovernmental democracy and human rights regimes in these regions will be in a gradual crossover process, as NGO networks pull government officials into "track two" (mixed government and NGO) dialogues and other informal exercises.

The Instrumental Effects of Globalization

In regions lacking a widespread and overt commitment to democracy, Western policymakers and nongovernmental groups trying to promote greater political liberalization have placed their faith in the indirect effects of globalization. In this view, globalization offers a bait and switch. An authoritarian government agrees to a global regime to gain benefits of one sort (usually economic) but is forced to accept the political consequences (greater popular pressure for democracy) that follow. Policies crafted in accord with this theory focus on two aspects of globalization—international trade liberalization and telecommunications. Not surprisingly, the theory also supports two cherished American beliefs: that open markets and democracy are the inspiration and consequence of one another and that the march of technology cannot be stopped.

Thus, for more than a decade successive U.S. administrations have claimed that broadly maintaining trade with China, and specifically encouraging China's entry into the World Trade Organization, would provide a back-door route to political reform. Adhering to WTO rules would require the regime in Beijing to provide more transparent and accountable government and would strengthen the concept of the rule of law, two fundamentals in modern democratic systems. In addition, foreign telecommunications companies would gain parity with government companies in China, spreading their technology and loosening the regime's control over contact between China and the outside world, as well as among Chinese citizens themselves.

The Limits of Globalization Logic

The logic, compelling in the long run, has short-term limits. In countries with enduring authoritarian regimes, leaders are more likely to accede to legal reform for pragmatic reasons—to improve economic conditions through increased international trade—so long as the reforms are not viewed by the populace as ideological capitulation. Leaders may also consider reforms pertaining to international trade to be easier to contain, because the initial focus is on commercial codes that primarily affect foreign business. Although it is possible to cordon off domestic populations in the early stages of such reform, the consequences of trade liberalization and marketization eventually require the regime to adopt a broader approach. But economic liberalization can also exacerbate problems that seem to outpace legal reform efforts and even encourage popular support for authoritarian or semi-authoritarian government. Russia's entry into the international economy has, in the minds of many Russians, worsened official corruption and economic crime. As long as these trends are perceived to be stronger than (even impervious to) reform, citizens are likely to tolerate less than democratic rule as a short-term solution.

Moreover, some of the economic powers poised to enter international trade regimes, most notably China, could themselves affect the rules governing those regimes. Thus far, global trade rules have largely been written by Western democracies, whose combined economic power has placed aspiring entrants in the role of supplicants. But the entry of more "mixed" economic powers—governments committed to market reform but not necessarily to Western-style democracy—may change these institutions. At the least, the link between trade preferences and transparent processes may weaken slightly, as may support for overt political conditionality linked to trade, in the mode of the European Union. At worst, global trade institutions could be rent with bloc behavior, not unlike that sometimes seen in the United Nations.

Technology and Political Openness

Technology's impact on democratization is likely to be more immediate, although not sufficient in itself to effect political change. Weak economies, along with government resistance, have contained the spread of technology in many Middle Eastern and some Asian states and will for the near future. But technology's advent has added a new dimension to the prospects for political change. The most dramatic episodes of popular resistance against authoritarian regimes in the past decade have featured prominent roles for technology. In Tiananmen Square in 1989, Chinese demonstrators communicated with one another and the outside world by fax. In Bangkok in 1992, Thai professionals, dubbed "mobile phone mobs," coordinated antimilitary demonstrations with student leaders and one another by cellular phone. In Indonesia in 1998, anti-Suharto resistance was largely directed via the Internet.

But for all these moments of high political drama, technology's greatest promise in promoting political openness lies in the everyday intercourse of civil and political life. In authoritarian societies, the Internet differs from print and electronic media, because no government-dominated media exist for the regime to use as a counterweight. From its inception, the Internet has been a freer form of communication than any other, at least for those able to obtain it.

Modernizing authoritarian states often wish to expand the use of technology for economic development but also to keep citizens from using it for political purposes. Doing both, however, is increasingly difficult. China's ambitious plan to build a national computerized information infrastructure has spurred domestic telecommunications industry growth of 30–50 percent a year since 1989. At the same time the government registers all Internet users, is investing in technology to monitor and filter cyber communications, and regulates acceptable topics for online discussion. But Chinese Internet users have learned how to circumvent many of these restrictions using proxy servers, a sign that technology can usually outmaneuver attempts to control it.

Today China's 17 million Internet users are a small fraction of the nation's population. But their number is increasing rapidly—growing 75 percent from 1997 to 1998 and then tripling in 1999. More important, political discourse in China has expanded despite state attempts to censor and prevent it. In the medium run, the effects of government efforts to control the Internet will depend in part on whether China can maintain brisk economic growth. If it does, Internet growth is likely to overwhelm attempts to control it. In the long run, the prognosis is favorable. In countries where technology is growing, control of global media may alternate between government and society, but the advantage will usually go to society in the end.

The Downsides for Democracy

But globalization can also hand authoritarian regimes an edge. Regimes that accede to economic reforms most often allow openings they are confident they can control. If the immediate impact is favorable—an improved economy, greater access to modern technology and goods—the regime's popular legitimacy may be strengthened by the perception that it has delivered (or at least permitted) the improvements. Ironically, globalization can thus extend the longevity of the regime, at least in the short run.

Conversely, bad economic times that are attributed, correctly or not, to globalization can also give authoritarian leaders a boost. When disillusionment with economic reform sets in, Western policy-makers' insistence on the link between reform and democratization can be used to authoritarian advantage. In the Asian economic crisis of 1997–98, Vietnam and Laos, which had begun very modest political reforms to accompany marketization, jettisoned these political moves when their trade with the countries hit hardest by the crisis declined. The failure of some of the region's fastest-growing economies—those linked most closely to the West—was taken as a warning of the dangers of globalization. Hard-liners eclipsed reformers in the early postcrisis years or replaced them altogether in the political structure.

Globalization has also helped sustain authoritarian regimes

by feeding nationalism in some non-Western states. During the Asian economic crisis, anti-Western sentiments flared even in countries well on the road to democracy, such as Thailand, when catastrophic drops in currency values were popularly attributed to manipulation by Western traders. In more authoritarian countries such as Malaysia, leaders turned this new nationalism to their advantage by salting their political platforms with anti-Western (and anti-globalization) rhetoric and portraying themselves as national champions.

Technology too has fed the nationalist backlash against globalization. Democracy promoters have long heralded the "CNN effect," in which television brings world events into the living rooms of people whose leaders would prefer to block such coverage. In Thailand in 1992, when the military government banned reports of Bangkok street demonstrations on government-owned television stations, coverage of the events (and the military crackdown on demonstrators) was transmitted to citizens through satellite television, creating a galvanizing force for resistance. In recent years, authoritarian regimes have used television to their own advantage. In 1999, satellite TV brought NATO's bombing of the Chinese embassy in Belgrade into the homes of urban Chinese, who were quick to respond with public protests. During that same incident nationalists also made use of the Internet. At the height of the protests, Chinese hackers broke into the website of the U.S. embassy in Beijing, in an eerie modern-day parallel to the 1900 Boxer Rebellion.

The New Global Elites?

Perhaps the most important impact of globalization on political reform, and one of the most difficult to foretell, will be the way it shapes new political and social classes, particularly in authoritarian countries. In recent decades social scientists have theorized that globalization—in particular its ability to improve economic conditions through trade—will help create new middle classes that will, in turn, increase pressure for democratic reform. There is some truth to this generalization, but it downplays the role of elites in political change. However strong popular pressure for democracy might be, a democratic transition usually requires the approval, overt or tacit, of a significant segment of the ruling order. The key question is not whether globalization can help serve up larger street crowds demanding change, but whether it can change the very nature of elite groups.

McMillan. © 2001 by Stephanie McMillan. Reproduced by permission.

Signs are emerging that globalization may be doing just that, with mixed effects for democratization. In countries (whether authoritarian or democratic) that emphasize modernization and economic growth based in part on foreign trade and investment, two developments are reshaping elite political culture. The first is the rise of technocrats, particularly those trained in global economics, in government and politics. In China, for example, technocrats are gradually assuming greater responsibility in the bureaucratic structure. The Communist Party of China has even begun to recruit them to enhance its own legitimacy. Technocrats are not, of course, automatically democratic reformers, but their influence can help make government more accountable and transparent, helping to lay the groundwork for a more democratic system.

A more noteworthy trend is the rise of new commercial elites in the power structures of many authoritarian and democratizing societies. Many made their fortunes in modern commercial sectors that benefited greatly from globalization. Seeking influence wherever they can find it, these new elites often pack the parliaments in countries where the executive branch had traditionally enjoyed exclusive control. In applying new communications techniques (and portions of their fortunes) to connect with voters, they have inspired a modern push for grassroots politics. Although generally considered reformers, they may also epitomize globalization's lack of regulation. As these new elites have assumed power, indictments for political corruption have increased.

Clearly, globalization is not a political panacea. At best a long-term ally in promoting democracy, it provides no automatic solutions. The sanguine correlations offered by some policymakers in the early post–Cold War years—particularly regarding the link between increased trade and democratization—should be reexamined. Although the advanced democracies can prime the pump of globalization, they should not expect to control the outcome or to realize immediate results. Indeed, the more enduring aspects of globalization may take at least a generation to realize. Until then, policymakers should be as ready to recognize globalization's costs to democratization as they are to laud its benefits.

Periodical Bibliography

The following articles have been selected to supplement the diverse views presented in this chapter.

Katharine Ainger — "Empires of the Senseless," *New Internationalist*, April 2001.

Stephen Bezruchka — "Is Globalization Dangerous to Our Health?" *Western Journal of Medicine*, May 2000.

Brian Campbell — "Globalization Myths and Reality," *Left Turn*, July/August 2002.

Cato Institute — "Globalization and Culture," *Cato Policy Report*, May/June 2003.

May H. Cooper — "World Trade: Is Globalization a Positive Trend?" *CQ Researcher*, June 9, 2000.

Tyler Cowen — "Does Globalization Kill Ethos and Diversity? *Phi Kappa Phi Forum*, Fall 2003.

P.J. Dinner — "Professor Debunks Globalization Myth," *Denver Business Journal*, November 30, 2001.

David P. Fidler — "The Return of 'Microbialpolitik,'" *Foreign Policy*, January/February 2001.

Ed Finn — "Corporate Globalization—Economically, Ecologically Disastrous," *Catholic New Times*, September 7, 2004.

Nick Gillespie — "Really Creative Destruction: Economist Tyler Cowen Argues for the Cultural Benefits of Globalization," *Reason*, August 2003.

Indur M. Goklany — "The Globalization of Human Well-Being," *CATO Policy Analysis*, August 22, 2002.

Ellen Goodman — "SARS and the Response," *Liberal Opinion Week*, May 12, 2003.

William Greider — "The Real Cancun: WTO Heads Nowhere," *Nation*, September 22, 2004.

Daniel T. Griswold — "The Best Way to Grow Future Democracies," *Philadelphia Inquirer*, February 15, 2004.

Naomi Klein — "Don't Fence Us In," *Guardian*, October 6, 2002.

Philippe Legrain — "Cultural Globalization Is Not Americanization," *Chronicle of Higher Education*, May 9, 2003.

Mike Miller — "Democracy Is Not a Spectator Sport," *Social Policy*, Summer 2002.

Joseph S. Nye Jr. — "Globalization Is About Blending, Not Homogenizing," *Washington Post*, October 14–20, 2002.

Vinoth Ramachandra — "Worldwide Inc.: When Global Meets Local, Who Wins?" *Sojourners*, April 2004.

Daniel Yergin — "Fighting the Globalization Flu," *Globalist Perspective*, May 29, 2004.

How Does Globalization Affect the Global Community?

Chapter Preface

Globalization is often defined as the increasing economic interdependence of countries. Some, however, define globalization more broadly. To the free flow of goods and capital, these analysts add the flow of people and ideas. They see an expanding global community, facilitated by technology, particularly the Internet. Kevin Kelly, a founding editor of *Wired*, claims, "One thousand years from now, when people write the history of this era, this will be remembered as the time when they wired up the planet and got it something like a central nervous system." Kelly adds, however, "When an organism starts to have a nervous system, it starts to feel pain and have doubts."

Serious doubts about the benefits of the free flow of people and information grew on September 11, 2001, when members of the terrorist group al Qaeda hijacked four commercial airliners, crashing two into the World Trade Center in New York City and a third into the Pentagon outside of Washington, D.C. The fourth crashed in a field near Shanksville, Pennsylvania. These attacks killed thousands. Former president Bill Clinton contends, "The terrorist attacks on September 11 were just as much a manifestation of this globalization and interdependence as the explosion of economic growth." For some analysts the spread of terrorism reveals an irony about the effects of globalization. While the free flow of ideas and people has increased worldwide access to democratic ideals, thus making many people less susceptible to the extremist ideologies of terrorists, it also allows terrorists to operate on a global scale. Indeed, terrorist organizations such as al Qaeda exploit the technologies that go hand in hand with globalization to plan their attacks.

The free flow of information and technology has created opportunities for terrorists to enter nations and coordinate terrorist attacks undetected. "As the world has now seen to its horror," *San Francisco Chronicle* editor Tom Abate argues, "these . . . empowering technologies [such as international travel and the Internet] enable tiny terrorist bands to wreak devastation on a scale never before imagined in human history." He adds, "The same technologies that empower our lives turn into double-edged swords in the wrong hands." Counterterrorist expert Jonathan Stevenson contends, for example, that because of technological advances al Qaeda needs no physical infrastructure. "Notebook computers, encryption, the Internet, multiple passports and the ease of global transportation enable al-Qaeda to function as a 'virtual' entity," Stevenson maintains. Al Qaeda's leader, Osama bin Laden, is particularly adroit at exploiting modern technology to his advantage. "The terrorist leader has mastered modern technologies and used the various circuits and switching points of globalization—mega-cities, international airports and harbors, skyscrapers, to name some—to invert and subvert the system," international relations professor Rajan Menon maintains.

The debate over whether globalization promotes or combats terrorism continues. The authors in the following chapter continue this discussion and also explore globalization's effects on war and the environment.

"Globalization promotes the conditions that lead to unrest, inequality, conflict, and, ultimately, war."

Globalization Promotes War

Steven Staples

Globalization creates the conditions that lead to war, argues Steven Staples in the following viewpoint. Multinational corporations exploit third world labor and resources, Staples claims, creating economic inequality and competition for diminishing environmental resources, the root causes of war. Moreover, he contends, globalization encourages nations to spend their resources on expensive militaries to protect the interests of international corporations. This provides these nations with the tools of war. Staples is chairman of the International Network on Disarmament and Globalization, a network of antiglobalization activists.

As you read, consider the following questions:

1. According to Staples, what evidence disproves the assertion that "all boats rise with the tide"?
2. In the author's opinion, why has the military-corporate complex of the new global economy replaced the military-industrial complex of the Cold War?
3. What is the next frontier to be made safe for corporations, according to U.S. military strategists?

Globalization and militarism should be seen as two sides of the same coin. On one side, globalization promotes the conditions that lead to unrest, inequality, conflict, and, ultimately, war. On the other side, globalization fuels the means to wage war by protecting and promoting the military industries needed to produce sophisticated weaponry. This weaponry, in turn, is used—or its use is threatened—to protect the investments of transnational corporations and their shareholders.

Inequality, Unrest, and Conflict

Economic inequality is growing; more conflict and civil wars are emerging. It is important to see a connection between these two situations.

Proponents of global economic integration argue that globalization promotes peace and economic development of the Third World. They assert that "all boats rise with the tide" when investors and corporations make higher profits. However, there is precious little evidence that this is true and substantial evidence of the opposite.

The United Nation's Human Development Report noted that globalization is creating new threats to human security. Economic inequality between Northern and Southern nations has worsened, not improved. There are more wars being fought today—mostly in the Third World—than there were during the Cold War. Most are not wars between countries, but are civil wars where the majority of deaths are civilians, not soldiers.

The mainstream media frequently oversimplify the causes of these wars, with claims they are rooted in religious or ethnic differences. A closer inspection reveals that the underlying source of such conflicts is economic in nature. Financial instability, economic inequality, competition for resources, and environmental degradation—all root causes of war—are exacerbated by globalization.

The Asian financial meltdown of 1997 to 1999 involved a terrible human cost. The economies of Thailand, South Korea, and Indonesia crumbled in the crisis. These countries, previously held up by neoliberal economists as the darlings of globalization, were reduced to riots and financial ruin.

The International Monetary Fund (IMF) stepped in to rescue foreign investors and impose austerity programs that opened the way for an invasion by foreign corporations that bought up assets devalued by capital flight and threw millions of people out of work. Political upheaval and conflict ensued, costing thousands of lives.

Meanwhile, other countries watched as their neighbors suffered the consequences of greater global integration. In India, citizens faced corporate recolonization, which spawned a nationalistic political movement. Part of the political program was the development of nuclear weapons—seen by many as the internationally accepted currency of power. Nuclear tests have put an already conflict-ridden region on the brink of nuclear war.

Fueling the Means to Wage War

The world economic system promotes military economies over civilian economies, pushing national economic policies toward military spending. The World Trade Organization (WTO), one of the main instruments of globalization, is largely based on the premise that the only legitimate role for a government is to provide for a military to protect the interests of the country and a police force to ensure order within. The WTO attacks governments' social and environmental policies that reduce corporate profits, and it has succeeded in having national laws that protect the environment struck down. Yet the WTO gives exemplary protection to government actions that develop, arm, and deploy armed forces and supply a military establishment. Article XXI of the General Agreement on Tariffs and Trade (GATT) allows governments free reign for actions taken in the interest of national security.

For example, in 1999 a WTO trade panel ruled against a Canadian government program that provided subsidies to aerospace and defense corporations for the production of civilian aircraft. Within weeks, the Canadian military announced a new $30 million subsidy program for the same Canadian corporations, but this time the money was for production of new weapons. In this case, the government was forced down the path of a military economy.

Contrast this WTO ruling with the billions of dollars the Pentagon gives to American weapons corporations for developing and producing military aircraft. The $309-billion U.S. military budget dwarfs the budgets of all its potential enemies combined, and with the collapse of the Soviet Union the U.S. faces no imminent military challengers. This large budget is, for all practical purposes, a corporate subsidy. Because the corporations involved happen to be building weapons, the subsidy is protected under GATT's Article XXI.

The use of military spending to develop a country's industrial and economic base has not been lost on Third World countries. Though struggling to lift itself from apartheid-era poverty and accompanying social problems, South Africa is spending billions of dollars on aircraft, warships, and even submarines in an effort to develop its economy.

South Africa stipulated that the arms it buys must be partially manufactured in South Africa. Finance Minister Trevor Manuel explained that the increase in military spending would allow "the National Defence Force to upgrade equipment, while providing a substantial boost to South African industry, foreign investment, and exports." South Africa's performance requirements would be wide open to WTO challenges if they were for building schools, hospitals, transportation infrastructure, or virtually anything except weapons.

South Africa is about to make the same mistake Northern industrialized countries made: it is creating new military projects that will become dependent on perpetual government funding, drawing money away from essential social programs. When the current weapons orders have been filled and government funding dries up, weapons corporations will have to find new customers to maintain current job levels, driving the arms trade and potentially causing a whole new arms race in the region.

The Military-Corporate Complex

Since the end of the Cold War, President [Dwight] Eisenhower's 1960s-era military-industrial complex has been fundamentally challenged by globalization. Globalization has weakened the powers of the nation-state, while freeing corporations to move profits and operations across national boundaries. Defense/military contractors, once considered part of the national industrial base and regulated and nurtured as such, are becoming detached from the nation-state and are able to pursue their interests independently.

Finding Profit in Poverty

Even as the influx of capital helps some countries prosper, it pulls others relentlessly toward war.

The lethal double dynamic begins with the dirt poor whom the spread of global capitalism has not helped. Half the planet lives on less than two dollars a day, a billion people on half that. For them, globalization has meant little in terms of real income gain. Oxfam [a poverty relief organization] . . . determined that incomes for people in countries that are pursuing a global program grew just 1.5 percent. For one in three of these countries, incomes actually rose more slowly than in states that resisted reforms.

There's profit in all that poverty, and it is most cheaply extracted in the form of war. Africa's battles are fought by a labor pool whose wages average 65 cents a day. An enterprising warlord can buy hundreds of willing combatants for the cost of a single American marine. A low value on human life makes war an attractive option; most of the world's battles pit one group of profiteers fighting with cheap soldiers against another.

Ted C. Fishman, *Harper's*, August 2002.

Globalization and the transnationalization of defense/military corporations have replaced the military-industrial complex of the Cold War economy with a military-corporate complex of the new global economy. This is based upon the dominance of corporate interests over those of the state. The weakened state is no longer able to reign in weapons corporations and is trapped increasingly by corporate interests: greater military spending, state subsidies, and a liberalization of the arms trade. Increased military production and the proliferation of weaponry take place without considering the costs of militarization to international diplomacy and peace. In many industrialized nations, government military spending has increased since the end of the Cold War.

Lockheed Martin, Boeing, BAE/Systems (formerly British

Aerospace), Raytheon, Thomson-CSF, and DaimlerChrysler Aerospace are all part of the military-corporate complex. Formerly national in orientation, these corporations have become transnational, with enormous revenues and tremendous economic and political power. . . .

Until the late 1990s, transatlantic mergers of defense/military contractors had been prohibited by governments due to national security concerns. In 1999, however, the Pentagon admitted that U.S. and European mergers were inevitable and accorded national treatment to BAE Systems, allowing it to be awarded military contracts as if it were an American corporation.

These mergers produce ever-larger and more powerful weapons-producing corporations. These newly merged corporations are able to greatly influence, even dictate, government defense and military policy. Government regulations have been weakened or removed altogether. For example, export controls designed to prevent weapons from being sold to countries at war or to countries that violate human rights are narrowly interpreted so that they do not interfere with corporate profits. Foreign embassies and trade missions abroad are used to aid arms sales.

The Threat of Military Force

According to *New York Times* columnist Thomas Friedman, "the hidden hand of the market will never work without a hidden fist. McDonald's cannot flourish without McDonnell Douglas, the builder of the F-15. And the hidden fist that keeps the world safe for Silicon Valley's technologies is called the United States Army, Air Force, Navy, and Marine Corps."

Friedman illuminates the strategic relationship that exists between corporations and militaries. As globalization extends the reach of corporate interests around the world, a matching military capacity must be deployed to protect those interests. This is the underlying reason the U.S. military maintains the capacity to wage two major wars in different regions of the world simultaneously.

There is nothing new about Friedman's "hidden fist." Military supremacy has always been a prerequisite for economic integration into a sphere of influence or an empire.

One can see this in the settling of the New World, when the network of military forts and outposts suppressed First Nations peoples and opened North America for settlers, prospectors, and industry barons.

Outer space is the next frontier to be made safe for corporations, according to U.S. military strategists. In Vision for 2020, the U.S. Space Command revealed that the "U.S. Space Command [is] dominating the space dimensions of military operations to protect U.S. interests and investment."

Globalization is driving a global war economy and creating the conditions for tremendous loss of human life. Many writers and researchers have documented the decline in human rights, social justice, environmental standards, and democracy caused by globalization. The inevitable outcome of globalization will be more wars—especially in the Third World where globalization has its harshest effects. Meanwhile, the elites of the industrialized world are confident that the global economy will continue to provide them with wealth created from the resources and labor of the Third World. Their technologically advanced militaries will protect them and their investments, insulating them from the violent effects of globalization.

What is required is a complete reassessment of the current global economic system, with the goal of promoting genuine human security and development. Global financial institutions, such as the World Trade Organization, that do not promote these goals must be revised or scrapped completely and replaced with a system based upon principles of equity, peace, and democracy.

VIEWPOINT 2

"Free trade, free markets, and free peoples bring not only prosperity, but also peace."

Globalization Promotes Peace

Gerald P. O'Driscoll and Sara J. Cooper

According to Gerald P. O'Driscoll and Sara J. Cooper in the following viewpoint, studies show that countries participating in global trade are less likely to wage war on each other. In contrast, the authors contend, countries that have not integrated into the global economy are more likely to resolve disputes on the battlefield. Thus, O'Driscoll and Cooper conclude, the free trade and open markets that accompany globalization promote peace. O'Driscoll is a senior fellow at the Cato Institute, and Cooper is a trade policy analyst at the Heritage Foundation, both think tanks that support free markets.

As you read, consider the following questions:

1. According to O'Driscoll and Cooper, what do economic and political repression breed?
2. How do leaders of countries that produce terrorists avoid accepting responsibility for policies that impoverish their own people, in the authors' view?
3. What do experts say is the primary factor responsible for five decades of peace in western Europe, in the authors' opinion?

Gerald P. O'Driscoll and Sara J. Cooper, "Trade Brings Security," *Orange County Register*, February 11, 2003.

Here's a fact that could throw a wrench into the next anti-globalization march (and the next call to arms): The free trade that protestors decry promotes more than just prosperity. A growing body of research suggests it also promotes something much closer to their hearts: Peace.

The evidence has become so strong that President [George W.] Bush has used it to show why a liberal trade policy is a necessary part of a strong national defense. The latest "National Security Strategy of the United States of America" says free trade and open markets can be as important to securing the peace for the long run as robust military funding.

The Danger of Economic Repression

The document represents new thinking in the government that U.S. security depends on economic success in other countries, that economic and political repression breed poverty, frustration and resentment, and that open markets—as well as open governments and open societies—can alleviate the causes of the terrorist threat against the West.

It is not that poverty causes terrorism. The 19 hijackers of [the terrorist attacks of] Sept. 11 [2001] were chiefly middle class in origin, with 15 coming from oil-rich Saudi Arabia. But the conditions that produce poverty—lack of economic freedom—also produce the sense of hopelessness and despair that breeds resentment.

Terrorist organizations exploit the situation to recruit new members. Meanwhile, the leaders of these countries blame the United States rather than accept responsibility for the policies impoverishing their own people.

As the Bush administration put it in its National Security Strategy document, "economic growth supported by free trade and free markets creates new jobs and higher incomes. It allows people to lift their lives out of poverty, spurs economic and legal reform, and the fight against corruption, and it reinforces the habits of liberty."

Helping the poor of the world prosper and reinforcing "the habits of liberty" certainly is an attractive alternative to a permanent war against radical Islam. And it would be far less costly.

Despite exceptions, such as Bahrain, most states in the

Middle East produce little economic growth for their populations. Even the vast oil supplies usually benefit only the elite.

The Link Between Globalization and Peace

Critics of globalization not only forget both the benefits of free trade and globalization for developing countries and for their poor and underemployed workers and the benefits of free trade to consumers everywhere, but they know almost nothing about the international-security benefits of free trade. Quantitative research has established the viability and prospect of a capitalist peace based on the following causal links between free trade and the avoidance of war: first, there is an indirect link running from free trade or economic openness to prosperity and democracy and ultimately to the democratic peace; second, trade and economic interdependence by themselves reduce the risk of military conflict. By promoting capitalism, economic freedom, trade, and prosperity, we simultaneously promote peace.

Erich Weede, *Independent Review*, Fall 2004.

A report by the World Bank says that 2 billion people—most of them in sub-Saharan Africa, the Middle East and the former Soviet Union—"live in countries that are being left behind." These countries have failed to integrate with the world economy, failed to knock down barriers to trade and investment flows, failed to establish property rights and, as a result, failed to grow into modern economies.

The Benefits of Economic Freedom

And, according to research by Edward Mansfield of the University of Pennsylvania and Jon Pevehouse of the University of Wisconsin, that's a recipe for trouble. Mansfield and Pevehouse have demonstrated that trade between nations makes them less likely to wage war on each other—and keeps internecine spats from spiraling out of control. They also found these trends are more pronounced among democratic countries with a strong tradition of respect for the rule of law.

Countries that trade with each other are far less likely to confront each other on the battlefield than are countries with no trade relationship. And the size of the economies involved doesn't affect this relationship, which means small, weak countries can enhance their defense capabilities simply by increasing trade with the world's economic giants.

Experts, including Mansfield and Pevehouse, say intensive trade integration, perhaps more than any other factor, has led to an unprecedented five decades of peace in Western Europe.

The countries of North and South America, they determined, generally have sought to integrate their economies in a variety of trade alliances, and international disputes on both continents tend to have been resolved without war. Conversely, countries of the Middle East and Africa, as well as Eastern Europe, historically have been less active in establishing trade relationships—and more active on the battlefield.

Trade is no substitute for a strong national defense, but the latter can't guarantee security on its own. Free trade, free markets, and free peoples bring not only prosperity, but also peace. And that's a goal shared by those who believe in globalization—and those who don't.

VIEWPOINT

"Many of the environmental and social problems that result from globalization are inherent in the model."

Globalization Is Harmful to the Environment

Jerry Mander

Global corporations lower those local environmental standards that restrict global economic growth, Jerry Mander maintains in the following viewpoint. As a result, these corporations are able to exhaust nations' resources and pollute with impunity, he asserts. Increased trade between nations also increases the need for global transport, he argues, which in turn increases fossil fuel usage. Mander, president of the International Forum on Globalization, is author of *The Case Against the Global Economy: And for a Turn Toward the Local.*

As you read, consider the following questions:

1. In Mander's opinion, how are earlier versions of global trade different from the modern version of economic globalization?
2. What is produced by the process of challenging democratically created laws and standards, in the author's view?
3. According to the author, how much of the world's water goes to industrial agriculture?

Jerry Mander, "The Environment and Globalization," *IFG Bulletin*, vol. 3, Summer 2002, pp. 1–3, 43.

Among many preposterous claims, advocates of economic globalization argue that the model increases long-term environmental protection. The theory goes that as countries globalize—often by exploiting resources like forests, minerals, oil, coal, fish, wildlife and water—their increased wealth will enable them to save more patches of nature from their ravages. Once they have reaped great profits, they will be able to introduce technical devices to mitigate the negative environmental impacts of their own increased production. The evidence suggests, however, that most of the benefit goes to global corporations, who have little incentive to put their profits into environmental improvements.

Many of the environmental and social problems that result from globalization are inherent in the model. No "side agreements" or techno-fixes will solve these problems. They are intrinsic to the form. We may have to change the form.

Nature or Nurture?

Advocates of economic globalization prefer to describe it as an inevitable process, the result of uncontrollable economic and technological forces that have simply evolved over centuries to their present form; that it's utopian to believe otherwise. Of course, if we accepted this description of the inevitability of it all as most media, governments, and universities tend to do, then obviously there would be no resistance possible and no point in talking about it. Our only option would be to lie there, watch TV, and submit, or else try somehow to take advantage of it for our own purposes.

Of course it's true enough that global trade has indeed existed for centuries in various forms. But earlier versions were entirely different from the modern version in scale, speed, form, impact and most importantly intent. The modern version of economic globalization was created by human beings, on purpose, and with a specific goal: to give primacy to economic—more correctly, corporate—values, above all others, and to aggressively install and codify those values globally. It was not inevitable, and it can be reversed or revised.

Globalization, as now designed, works to integrate and merge all economic activity on the planet within a single homogenized model of development that directly serves the efficiency needs of the largest corporations by allowing them to duplicate their production and marketing efforts on an ever expanding terrain. Primary importance is given to the achievement of economic *hypergrowth*, fueled by the constant search for access to new resources, new and cheaper labor sources, and new markets. It is the job of instruments of globalization such as the World Trade Organization (WTO) the World Bank, the International Monetary Fund (IMF), etc., to assist these processes by creating rules that require nations to conform to these principles, while eliminating impediments within individual nations that might restrict corporate access to markets, labor, and resources. In practice, unfortunately, most of these so called impediments are laws created by governments, which are nonetheless viewed by free traders as "non-tariff barriers to trade" and are subject to WTO challenges.

Challenging the Environment

Though it is only seven years old, the WTO already has an impressive record for challenging democratically created laws and standards. It's been particularly potent in the environmental realm. The WTO's very first ruling was against a portion of the U.S. Clean Air Act, which set high standards against polluting gasoline. A section of the Act was found to be noncompliant with WTO trade rules and, like so many standards since, had to be softened. In agriculture areas, the WTO has ruled in favor of large machine and chemical intensive global industrial agriculture corporations over small-scale family farming, and indigenous farmers—most appallingly in the famous Chiquita banana case. That case held that the European Union could not favor small indigenous, often organic, farmers within former European colonies, over the industrial bananas from Chiquita.

The way these challenges work is really interesting. Almost always, countries challenge other countries' trade rules on behalf of global corporations. So the U.S. sues to protect Chiquita bananas, and Venezuela sues to protect its oil industry, and Mexico sues to protect its tuna industry. The whole process produces a mutual ratcheting downward of environmental, labor, and health standards. It's a way that corporations can get their own governments to destroy laws in other countries, just as they pressure for deregulation domestically. The result is that all laws and standards race downward to a low common denominator, just as is happening with global wage standards.

This is not to mention a secondary "chilling effect" from this process. For example, Canada cancelled its national ban on the gasoline additive "MMT," a well-known carcinogen, under threat of suit through the North American Free Trade Agreement (NAFTA).

The Consequences of Increased Global Transport

Arguably the most important principle of free trade is its emphasis on global conversion to *export-oriented production.* The central feature of an export-oriented model is obviously that it increases transport and shipping activity. Minneapolis economist, David Morris, loves to use the example of a toothpick, which comes wrapped in plastic, and is marked, "Made in Japan." Japan is skilled in industrial production, but it has very few trees, and no oil. But in a global economy, it is somehow thought efficient to ship wood from a country that has it—Chile, Canada, the U.S.—and also to ship barrels of oil to Japan, then wrap the one in the other, package them in serviceable commodity units, and ship them back across oceans to consumers. That toothpick, by the time it is finally used, might have traveled 50,000 miles. Similarly, ingredients in the average plate of food on American dinner tables these days is estimated to travel on the average about 1,500 miles from source to plate.

As global transport increases, it requires massive increase in global infrastructure development. This is good for large corporations like Bechtel, who get to do the construction work. But it's bad news for the environments where new airports, seaports, oilfields, pipelines for the oil, rail lines and high speed highways are needed. Many of these things are built in wilderness or forested areas with previously intact biodiversity, coral reefs, rural areas, etc.

Even more important is the increase of fossil fuel use. Ocean shipping carries nearly 80 percent of the world's international trade in goods, and projections indicate major growth over the next few years. The fuel that's commonly used is a mixture of diesel and low quality oil known as "Bunker C," which is particularly polluting.

Increased air transport is even worse than shipping. One physicist at Boeing once described the pollution from the take-off of a single 747 as being like "setting the local gas station on fire and flying it over your neighborhood." A two-minute take-off of a 747 is equal to 2.4 million lawn-mowers running for 20 minutes. It's now estimated that the increase of global transport is one of the largest contributors to the growing crisis of climate change.

Pushing the Earth to the Brink

Corporate globalization, with its mandate to put profit first, above both planet and people, has pushed the life support systems of the Earth to the brink of collapse. This ecological crisis makes it increasingly obvious that an economic system based on the accumulation of wealth and unlimited growth is incompatible with our finite planet. The transformation of virgin forests, pristine rivers, etc. into "resources" is simply not sustainable.

Global Justice Ecology Project, "Corporate Globalization, War and the Environment: It's All One Struggle," April 3, 2004. www.globaljusticeecology.org.

Connected to global transport is the epidemic increase of bioinvasions, a major cause of species extinction. With the growth of global transport, billions of creatures are on the move. From viruses to rats; from bacteria to mosquitoes; from nematodes to exotic seeds; all are getting free transport in the global economy, and many are thriving in their new homes, often outcompeting native species, and bringing pollution or health crises.

There is no way around the problem. If you are going to design a system built on the premise that dramatically increased global trade is good, you are going to increase transport activity and you are guaranteed to bring on these kinds of problems, and many more. They are intrinsic to the model.

Creating Hunger and Ecological Destruction

Industrial agriculture is said to be efficient and to produce cheaper food, but these claims are false. This is a kind of efficiency that ignores the costs of air, water, and soil pollution; toxic rivers and dead fish; the loss of topsoil from heavy pesticide and machine intensive production, and the increased use of fossil fuels. Although their numbers are dwindling, nearly half of the world's population is small farmers. With their intimate knowledge of local crops and how to breed for local soils and climate, how to minimize insect blights and keep soil productive, they feed their families, communities and local and regional markets. However, through the new industrial agriculture system, often run by global transnational corporations, farms are bought up and merged into huge ones. They eliminate diverse cropping and substitute single-crop monocultures for the export market.

Eventually, the farmers and their families are forced to flee to crowded urban slums where they compete for rare, poorly paid urban jobs. Families that once fed themselves become society's burden, while huge agribusinesses profit.

The environmental problems that are intrinsic to this shift to industrial agriculture are immense. By definition, monocultural production drastically reduces biodiversity, not only by killing the microscopic life within the soils through heavy chemical use, but also by reducing production of commodities to one or two export varieties. Where indigenous Filipinos, for example, once grew thousands of varieties of rice, now two varieties account for 98 percent of production, and the other varieties are disappearing. According to the Food and Agriculture Organization (FAO) of the United Nations (UN), the world has already lost up to 75 percent of its crop diversity because of the globalization of industrialized agriculture.

Taking all these external social and environmental costs into account, is it not preposterous to call this system efficient? Maybe you can get a tomato from Mexico at a few cents less at the store, but we all pay more in higher taxes in future years to clean up the messes this system causes. In the end, however, the environment pays the most.

Now companies offer biotech as a "clean" solution. Corporations patent indigenous varieties of seeds that communities of farmers have developed for millennia, and genetically alter seeds so they will not reproduce—these are so-called "terminator" seeds—thus assuring that farmers must buy new seeds annually from the corporations. Does anyone really believe this has something to do with feeding the hungry? That's just their advertising slogan.

The Commodification of Water

The UN reports that now more than one billion people on earth lack access to clean drinking water. Population growth is not the major problem—the rate of increase in water use is twice the rate of population growth. Why? People only use about 15 percent of the global fresh water supply, however 65 percent goes to industrial agriculture (which uses it at a much higher rate than do small farms) and to high tech production, especially for computer chip manufacture, which requires absolutely pure water.

One would expect governments and global bureaucracies to advocate conservation. Instead what's being proposed is to privatize, commodify, and globalize the planet's remaining fresh water—its lakes, rivers, streams—to sell exploitation rights to corporations, and let the global market decide who gets to drink it or use it. Most of the water goes to industrial users once water systems are fully privatized and globalized—a process that is being massively aided by the new General Agreement on Trade in Services (GATS), as well as the Free Trade Area of the Americas (FTAA). Most of the people on the planet who are actually thirsty, will not be able to pay for it. Who gets the scarce water—Bill Gates or the peasants in Bolivia?

VIEWPOINT

"Environmental advocates should embrace global wealth creation as a fundamental strategy for achieving environmental sustainability."

Globalization Benefits the Environment

John A. Charles

In the following viewpoint John A. Charles argues that globalization promotes environmental sustainability. Charles refutes claims that an open economy is unsustainable. For example, Charles maintains, in the United States energy consumption has dropped and air and water quality have improved, all signs that the U.S. economy is environmentally sustainable. Moreover, he claims, affluent societies demand environmental protections, and since globalization promotes wealth, more free markets will in turn promote environmental improvements worldwide. Charles is environmental policy director at Cascade Policy Institute, which advances policies that foster individual liberty, personal responsibility, and economic opportunity in Oregon.

As you read, consider the following questions:

1. According to Charles, what is the most direct measure of sustainability?
2. What is the relationship between per capita income and certain kinds of pollution, according to the World Bank?
3. In the author's opinion, what has research shown about foreign and domestic plants in some sections of some developing countries?

John A. Charles, "The Environmental Benefits of Globalization," *Oregon's Future*, vol. 4, Spring 2003.

Environmental activists who criticize free trade often make two arguments. First, they criticize the American lifestyle as environmentally "unsustainable" and fear that adoption of similar values by other cultures through globalization would result in catastrophic shortages of finite natural resources. As summarized by environmental writer Alan Thein Durning, "if people in 3rd World countries lived the same lifestyle as the average American, we'd need seven more earths" to provide all the natural resources.

The second argument is that international trade encourages multi-national corporations to shop for the locations offering the weakest environmental protections, fostering a "race to the bottom" that puts profits ahead of all other values.

While these are legitimate concerns, there is little evidence to support either argument.

Is the American Lifestyle Unsustainable?

Many "sustainability" advocates start from the premise that an open, dynamic economy is inherently unsustainable because producers and consumers are primarily concerned with their own self-interest. Without a centralized control mechanism, it is argued, the economy expands infinitely while the earth's resources are finite. Thus, promoting capitalism on a global scale will only accelerate the process towards eventual collapse.

Fortunately, empirical trends of the past 50–75 years suggest a very different conclusion. Economic indicators show that the U.S. economy is becoming steadily more efficient and less polluting over time, and there is no reason this trend should not continue indefinitely.

Measuring Sustainability

The most direct measure of sustainability is the amount of energy consumed per unit of economic output. If an economic system takes increasing amounts of energy over time to produce the same unit of output, then it's unlikely to sustain itself. On the other hand, an economy that actually does more with less energy each year is one that is built for the long haul.

The U.S. economy has shown a remarkable drop in energy

intensity during the past 50 years. Between 1949 and 2000, energy consumption per dollar of Gross Domestic Product (GDP) dropped steadily from 20.63 thousand Btu to 10.57. In other words, at the beginning of the new millennium, we were able to produce the same economic output that we had in 1949 using only half as much energy.

This is an important indicator of sustainability, but there are many others as well:

- *Air quality.* Between 1970 and 1997, U.S. population increased 31 percent, vehicle miles traveled increased 127 percent, and gross domestic product increased 114 percent—yet total air pollution actually decreased by about 31 percent.
- *Water quality.* In 1972, approximately 36% of American streams were usable for fishing and/or swimming. This had increased to 64% by 1982 and 85% by 1994.
- *Timber supply.* The net growth of timber has exceeded the levels of timber harvest every decade since 1952. According to the U.S. Forest Service, we currently grow about 22 million net new cubic feet of wood per year, while harvesting only about 16.5 million, a net increase of 36% annually.
- *Agricultural production.* In the past 30 years, the production of food grains in the United States increased by 82%, while the amount of land used for growing remained relatively constant. Planted areas for all crops today in the U.S. is actually lower than it was in 1930; this has freed up land for other non-commodity uses such as wildlife habitat and outdoor recreation.
- *Availability of mineral resources.* Resources that were once considered scarce are now known to be abundant. Between 1950 and 2000, the proven reserves of bauxite went up 1,786%. Reserves of chromium increased 5,143%, and quantities of copper, iron ore, nickel, tin and zinc all went up by more than 125%. The 1970s forecasts of doom for oil proved to be spectacularly wrong; the retail price of gasoline in the late 1990's (adjusted for inflation) was cheaper than at any time in history.

The rise in living standards has had tremendous public health benefits as well. The infant mortality rate in the United

States dropped from 29.2 per thousand in 1950 to 7.1 in 1997. Since 1980, the death rate for cancer has dropped more than 11% for individuals between the ages of 25 and 64. As a result of these and other similar trends, the life expectancy for all Americans rose from 70.8 years in 1970 to 75.8 by 1995.

Wealthier Is Healthier

Although it's counter-intuitive to many environmental advocates, rising affluence is an important prerequisite to environmental improvement. Empirical research first published in 1992 by the World Bank showed that the statistical relationship between per capita income and certain kinds of pollution is roughly shaped as an inverted U. In other words, economic growth is bad for air and water pollution at the initial stages of industrialization, but later on reduces pollution as countries become rich enough to pay for control technologies.

Wealth creation also changes consumer demand for environmental quality. The richer people become, the more they tend to value environmental objectives such as safe drinking water, proper sewage disposal, and clean air. Once these basic needs are met, they begin raising the bar by demanding such "amenities" as scenic vistas and habitat for non-game wildlife. As their income rises, they increasingly have the financial resources to act on these values by imposing appropriate regulations on polluters and purchasing technologies that provide environmental benefits.

A recent report by the World Trade Organization reinforces these points. The report concludes:

> One reason why environmental protection is lagging in many countries is low incomes. Countries that live on the margin may simply not be able to afford to set aside resources for pollution abatement. . . . If poverty is at the core of the problem, economic growth will be part of the solution, to the extent that it allows countries to shift gears from more immediate concerns to long run sustainability issues. Indeed, at least some empirical evidence suggests that pollution increases at the early stages of development but decreases after a certain income level has been reached. . . .

Many so-called "sustainability" advocates argue for greater central control of the economy through government intervention, but every place this has been tried has proven

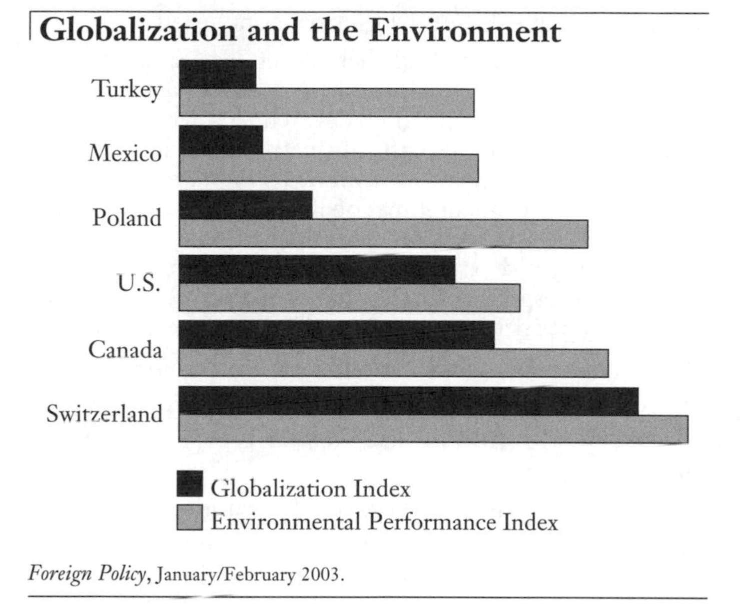

Globalization and the Environment

Foreign Policy, January/February 2003.

to be a failure. Some of the most polluted cities on the face of the earth are in countries formerly or currently under socialist rule. Leaders of the former Soviet Union and East Germany were as confident in their ability to run the economy as local sustainable development advocates are in Oregon, but they found out that eliminating market competition also eliminated incentives to develop innovative technologies that use resources more efficiently.

Does Free Trade Promote an Environmental "Race to the Bottom"?

It's often asserted by trade critics that multi-national corporations, if unrestrained by government oversight, will shop around for countries with lax environmental regulations. This will exert a downward pressure on pollution control efforts, fostering an environmental "race to the bottom".

There is little evidence to support this hypothesis. Studies have shown that such issues as access to markets and labor costs are far more important to companies looking to locate new facilities. When those new facilities are built, there are many reasons why managers tend to maintain high environmental standards, even when not required to do so. As a study by Daniel Esty and Bradford Gentry concluded:

> First, many companies find that the efficiency of having a single set of management practices, pollution control technologies, and training programs geared to a common set of standards outweigh any cost advantage that might be obtained by scaling back on environmental investments at overseas facilities. Second, multinational enterprises often operate on a large scale, and recognize that their visibility makes them especially attractive targets for local enforcement officials. . . . Third, the prospect of liability for failing to meet standards often motivates better environmental performance. . . .

Other research has shown that, within given sectors in given developing countries, foreign plants are significantly more energy efficient and use cleaner types of energy than domestic plants.

It is human nature to seek out others and exchange ideas, products and services. Attempting to limit that impulse, whether in the name of environmental sustainability, fighting communism, or some other moral crusade, is likely to be a costly and futile undertaking. Perhaps nowhere has this been more vividly demonstrated than in Cuba, where the U.S. has enforced a trade embargo for more than 40 years. Despite the embargo, American consumer products are widely available in the Cuban underground economy, and American dollars tend to be the currency of choice. Meanwhile, the primary purpose of the embargo—to oust [Cuban premier] Fidel Castro—has obviously failed.

The evidence shows that our preference for free trade is not in conflict with our desire for environmental quality. On the contrary, income derived from free trade is a prerequisite for most types of environmental gain. Wealthier people place greater value on environmental amenities, and they have the resources to pay for them. True environmental advocates should embrace global wealth creation as a fundamental strategy for achieving environmental sustainability.

Periodical Bibliography

The following articles have been selected to supplement the diverse views presented in this chapter.

Tom Abate	"Silicon Valley Goes to War: Technology Has Two Faces as World Changes," *San Francisco Chronicle*, September 23, 2001.
Andrew Bernstein	"Global Capitalism: Curing Oppression and Poverty," *Freeman*, December 2003.
Kurt M. Campbell	"Globalization's First War?" *Washington Quarterly*, Winter 2002.
Ann Florini	"Is Global Civil Society a Good Thing?" *New Perspectives Quarterly*, Spring 2004.
Jeffrey A. Frankel	"The Environment and Globalization," *Weatherhead Center for International Affairs*, May 2003.
Igor Ivanov	"International Security in the Era of Globalization," *Telegraph* (Katmandu), March 4, 2003.
Kelly Lawig	"Overcoming Globalization: The Root of Violence," *Ecumenical Review*, July 2003.
Akin L. Mabogunje	"Poverty and Environmental Degradation: Challenges Within the Global Economy," *Environment*, January/February 2002.
Jerry Mander	"Economic Globalization and the Environment," *Tikkun*, September/October 2001.
Rajah Menon	"Terrorism Inc.: Amid Globalization, Al Qaeda Looks a Lot Like GM," *Los Angeles Times*, August 22, 2004.
Ludwig von Mises	"The Economic Causes of War," *Freeman*, April 2004.
Carl Pope	"Race to the Top: The Biases of the WTO Regime," *Harvard International Review*, Winter 2002.
Bob Wallace	"The Free Market Is the Best Weapon Against Terrorism," *LewRockwell.com*, October 16, 2001.
Erich Weede	"The Diffusion of Prosperity and Peace by Globalization," *Independent Review*, Fall 2004.
Robert B. Zoellick	"Countering Terror with Trade," *Washington Post*, September 20, 2001.

Chapter 3

How Does Globalization Affect Developing Nations?

Chapter Preface

Women in the developing world play a major role in globalization. According to Women's Edge, an organization that advocates international economic policies that support women in the developing world, "When we talk about the global economy, women really are a major part of it. They are the majority of the workers in factories and the majority of farmers around the world. They grow 50 percent of the food that we all eat. As international trade impacts those areas of manufacturing, production, farming, it significantly impacts women." Because women in developing nations play such a significant role in global trade, one controversy in the debate over the impact of globalization on developing nations is whether globalization has a positive or a negative effect on the women who live and work in these countries.

Some analysts claim that globalization has a positive impact on women in the developing world. They argue that in developing nations, where historically women have been repressed, economic globalization may have liberating effects. Pete Geddes, program director of Foundation for Research on Economics and the Environment, asserts, "Globalization has rapidly improved the social and economic status of women in the developing world. The explanation is straightforward. In a competitive, globalized world, the role of women becomes ever more valuable. Cultures that exclude women from full participation (e.g. Saudi Arabia) fall ever further behind." Indeed, when women are prohibited from working or joining certain professions, nations lose the benefits of their labor and are less able to compete with countries that take advantage of women's contributions. In addition, some women's rights advocates see the globalization of information, particularly via the Internet, as an ally in the fight for women's rights worldwide. Activist Jessica Neuwirth contends,

> Action alert campaigns to protect women from being stoned, flogged, and mutilated have been exponentially amplified through the use of e-mail, as have interventions demanding justice for women who have been raped, beaten, or killed with impunity. On-line campaigns—protesting the systematic destruction of women through gender apartheid in Afghanistan . . . and the detrimental role played by UN peacekeeping mis-

sions in promoting prostitution and trafficking—have raised awareness of these issues and generated public pressure to stop human-rights violations against women.

Some commentators claim, however, that globalization has in the main had a negative impact on women in the developing world. Because women in developing nations comprise the largest percentage of workers in the factories of global corporations, in many ways these women drive globalization. Nevertheless, they have not received its benefits, argues Bonnie Block, former chair of the Wisconsin Network for Peace and Justice. "Women and girls own less than 1% of the planet's wealth; they furnish 70% of the work hours and receive only 10% of the income," Block maintains. Poor working conditions are an oft-cited example of the negative impact of globalization on women in developing nations. Laws that ensure a fair wage and safe workplace conditions increase the cost of doing business at the expense of profits. Profits are thus greater for companies operating in developing nations that have no such laws, and this advantage is attractive to foreign investors. Large export factories, often managed by global corporations, pay low wages for long hours worked in unsafe conditions. "Women make up much of the underpaid workforce in these areas where regulations and labour protection laws are relaxed or not enforced in order to attract foreign investors," maintains Women and the Economy, a women's rights organization. "Women's nimble fingers," they add, "are in high demand as vegetable packers in Mexico, garment workers in China, and cotton harvesters in Egypt. These are all industries characterized by low wages, and poor working conditions including long hours, lack of safety standards, and barriers to workers organizing."

The contradictions inherent in globalization, particularly for women in the developing world, remain. "Although to date globalization has magnified the power differentials that subordinate women," Neuwirth suggests, "it also creates an urgent need for fundamental political reform, and thus represents an opportunity to reorder the world in a way that serves humanity—and particularly the female majority of humanity—better."

1

VIEWPOINT

"The losers in the age of globalization are the countries that refuse to embrace economic liberalization and the global market."

Globalization Helps Developing Nations

Brett D. Schaefer

Developing nations that participate in the global marketplace experience economic growth and prosperity, argues Brett D. Schaefer in the following viewpoint. The resulting prosperity in turn improves labor and environmental standards in developing countries, Schaefer claims. However, he asserts, only developing nations with governments and institutions that uphold human rights and invest in health and education will experience these benefits. Schaefer is a fellow in international regulatory affairs at the Heritage Foundation, a think tank that supports free enterprise and limited government.

As you read, consider the following questions:

1. What evidence does Schaefer cite to support his view that U.S. aid has not led to strong economic growth in all countries that receive aid?
2. In the author's opinion, why does a relationship exist between economic freedom and per capita income?
3. What reality about reform does the Millennium Challenge Account recognize, in the author's view?

Brett D. Schaefer, "Promoting Growth and Prosperity in the Developing World Through Economic Freedom," *Economic Perspectives*, vol. 8, March 2003.

For over 50 years, developed nations have spent hundreds of billions of dollars in multilateral and bilateral assistance trying to help poor countries develop. The record of this effort is very disappointing. Aid has more often been ineffective or counterproductive than it has achieved its intended goal of spurring economic growth and development. As a result, poverty remains among the world's most pressing problems, and many recipients of development assistance are today as poor or poorer than they were decades ago.

The Failure of Development Assistance

To many governments and non-governmental organizations, this failing is due in large part to insufficient development assistance. For instance, after President [George W.] Bush's pledge to increase the United States' development assistance budget by $5 billion annually through the Millennium Challenge Account, the Center for Global Development and the Center on Budget and Policy Priorities criticized:

"The level of spending proposed by the Bush Administration . . . would still leave aid spending as a share of all government spending and as a share of the economy well below its historical averages."

But the failure of development assistance is not due to a lack of resources. For instance, Organization for Economic Cooperation and Development (OECD) data show that between 1980 and 2000 the United States alone gave over $144 billion (in constant 1999 U.S. dollars) in official development assistance to 97 countries, regions, and territories for which per capita gross domestic product (GDP) data from 1980 to 2000 are available.

These 97 countries had a median inflation-adjusted per capita GDP of $1,076 in 1980 but only $994 in 2000, a decline in real terms.

Compound annual growth in per capita GDP for these countries averaged 0.16 percent, with 12 experiencing negative growth and only four achieving growth over 1 percent.

Clearly, development assistance did not uniformly or frequently lead to strong economic growth. As noted by former World Bank economist William Easterly in his article "The Cartel of Good Intentions," "as many aid-receiving low-income countries had negative per capita growth as positive. . . . Among all low-income countries, there is not a clear relationship between aid and growth." What is clear from this experience is that simply increasing investment through foreign assistance will not promote growth and prosperity in developing countries.

The Path to Growth and Prosperity

Economic studies, conceding that the level of aid is not the central issue, have focused on what policies are most conducive to economic growth and development. In its *1996 World Development Report: From Plan to Market* the World Bank observed,

> The state-dominated economic systems of [developing and former Communist] countries, weighted down by bureaucratic control and inefficiency, largely prevented markets from functioning and were therefore incapable of sustaining improvements in human welfare.

Subsequent World Bank studies have demonstrated that open markets and economic liberalization provide the fastest, most reliable path to increased growth and prosperity. A 2002 World Bank study titled *Globalization, Growth, and Poverty: Building an Inclusive World Economy* found that increased globalization (defined as trade as a percentage of GDP) from the late 1970s to the late 1990s led to higher economic growth. The more globalized developing countries (24 developing countries with over 3 billion people) achieved average growth in income per capita of 5 percent per year in the 1990s. By contrast, in less globalized developing countries "aggregate growth rate was actually negative in the 1990s." The losers in the age of globalization are the countries that refuse to embrace economic liberalization and the global market.

Contrary to the claims often raised by anti-globalization activists, World Bank analysis found that globalization helps the poor as much as the rich and improves labor and environmental standards in the long run. A June 2001 World Bank study titled *Trade, Growth, and Poverty* found that increased growth resulting from "expanded trade leads to proportionate increases in incomes of the poor . . . globalization leads to faster growth and poverty reduction in poor countries." *Globalization, Growth, and Poverty* found that while wages may dip in the short term after liberalization, "in the long run workers gain from integration. Wages have grown twice as fast in the more globalized developing countries than in the less globalized ones, and faster than in rich countries as well." Similarly, "despite widespread fears, there is no evidence of a decline in environmental standards. In fact, a . . . study of air quality in major industrial centers of the new globalizers found that it had improved significantly in all of them."

The Relationship Between Globalization and Economic Freedom

The *Index of Economic Freedom*, published annually by the Heritage Foundation and the *Wall Street Journal*, confirms these studies. The *Index* grades 10 factors for 161 countries with 1 being the best score and 5 being the worst score. These factors are: trade policy, fiscal burden of government, government intervention in the economy, monetary policy, capital flows and foreign investment, banking and finance, wages and prices, property rights, regulation, and black market activity. Those 10 scores for these factors are then averaged to give an overall score for economic freedom. Countries are designated "free," "mostly free," "mostly unfree," and "repressed" based on these overall scores.

As shown in the *Index*, free countries on average have a per capita income twice that of mostly free countries, and mostly free countries have a per capita income more than three times that of mostly unfree and repressed countries. This relationship exists because countries maintaining policies that promote economic freedom provide an environment that facilitates trade and encourages entrepreneurial activity, which in turn generates economic growth.

Analysis by economists Richard Roll of University of California Los Angeles and John Talbott of the Global Development Group supports the conclusion that the path to increased growth and prosperity is for countries to adopt policies that promote economic freedom and the rule of law as measured by the *Index*. Their work demonstrates that the economic, legal, and political institutions of a country explain more than 80 percent of the international variation in real income per capita between 1995 and 1999 in more than 130 countries. Civil liberties, government expenditures, political rights, press freedom, and strong property rights had the most consistent, positive influence on a country's per capita income. The variables having a negative effect on per capita income included black market activity, excessive regulation, poor monetary policy, and trade barriers. Roll and Talbott found a strong relationship between economic freedom and the level of per capita income in a country, concluding that economic freedom is clearly important to a country's development:

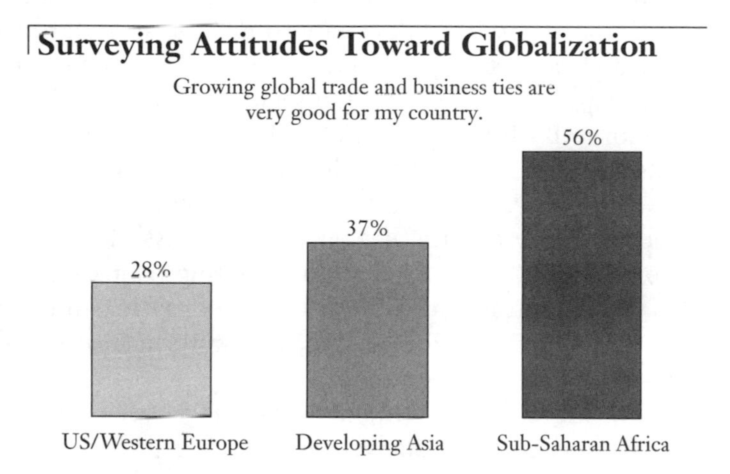

The Pew Global Attitudes Project, June 3, 2003. www.pewtrusts.com.

"Liberalizations are, on average, followed by dramatic improvement in country income, while substantial reductions in growth typically follow antidemocratic events. We conclude that countries can develop faster by enforcing strong property rights, fostering an independent judiciary, attacking corruption, dismantling burdensome regulation, allowing press freedom, and protecting political rights and civil liberties. These features define a healthy environment for economic activity. . . .

"Economic participants cannot save in a world of inflationary government-sponsored counterfeiting. They cannot compete with state-sponsored monopolies. They cannot trade efficiently with the existence of high tariffs and phony official exchange rates. They cannot easily overcome burdensome regulation and corruption. They cannot capitalize future profits in a world devoid of property rights. And they cannot prosper without economic and personal freedoms."

The study confirms that the rule of law and sound economic policies such as trade liberalization and low inflation are central to increased growth and prosperity.

Making Aid Work

The evidence thus indicates that economic assistance can only spur growth in countries with good economic policies and institutions—in bad policy environments, aid is far less effective and can actually be counterproductive. Taking this experience and analysis on development into account, President George Bush proposed a new development assistance program: The Millennium Challenge Account (MCA).

The MCA represents a fundamental revolution in development assistance because it would provide assistance only to countries with a proven record in adopting policies (good governance, rooting out corruption, upholding human rights, adhering to the rule of law, investing in health and education, and adopting sound economic policies that foster enterprise and entrepreneurship) that have been proven complementary and conducive to economic growth. This focus on policies that bolster economic growth is appropriate because increased prosperity allows parents the luxury of educating their children instead of making them work to help provide for their families. Prosperity enables individuals to value green spaces for their aesthetic value rather than their potential as fields for crops or trees for fuel. It permits the workforce to worry about the quality of the work environment rather than the lack of employment. And prosperity gives families the means to engage in preventive health practices that lead to longer lives.

Similarly, a fair, strong, and reliable rule of law is necessary to give people the confidence to make long-term investments to improve their lives without fear that those investments will be arbitrarily taken from them. As noted by Peruvian economist Hernando de Soto in *The Mystery of Capital*,

> The poor inhabitants of [developing and former communist nations]—five-sixths of humanity—do have things, but they lack the process to represent their property and create capital. They have houses but not titles; crops but not deeds; businesses but not statutes of incorporation. . . . The total value of the real estate held but not legally owned by the poor of the Third World and former communist nations is at least $9.3 trillion.

It is the absence of the rule of law that keeps the poor from utilizing these assets for their own benefit.

The MCA is humble in its approach because it accepts that aid alone will not result in increased growth and prosperity and recognizes that bilateral or multilateral donors cannot force a developing country government to embrace reform against its will. A weakness of prior development efforts was trying to force reform. The difficulty of forcing governments to adopt reform is evident in the frequent failures of the International Monetary Fund (IMF) and the World Bank to impose conditionality on recipients. History shows that governments of recipient countries often pledge more than they deliver in return for IMF and World Bank assistance—a conclusion supported by World Bank analysis in *Assessing Aid: What Works, What Doesn't, and Why*, which found "conditionality is unlikely to bring about lasting reform if there is no strong domestic movement for change." The MCA recognizes that reform must be home grown if it is to endure for the long-term. Due to this reality, President Bush's insistence that the MCA should focus its resources on developing countries that have a proven track record in the policies conducive to development may be the most important aspect of the program. Instead of granting assistance to elicit reform, the program will grant assistance to countries that have already demonstrated a willingness to reform, thereby increasing the odds that those funds will be effective.

A New Opportunity for Growth and Prosperity

The important lessons here are plain. First, increasing economic growth and individual prosperity through economic freedom must be core goals of development. Second, economic assistance can improve economic growth only in good policy environments. Third, the economic futures of developing countries lie predominantly in their own hands through the policies that they choose to adopt and enforce—long-term policy reform cannot be forced upon them.

By requiring aid recipients to prove their adherence to the policies proven to catalyze development, the MCA constitutes a welcome recognition of the limitations of development assistance while maintaining the spirit of aid by offering a helping hand to the nations striving to help themselves.

VIEWPOINT 2

"Small farmers . . . are the immediate and dramatic victims of globalization but the damage is far more widespread."

Globalization Has Harmed Developing Nations

Lila Rajiva

In the following viewpoint Lila Rajiva, an Indian immigrant living in the United States, contends that multinational corporations, not developing nations, are the primary beneficiaries of globalization. In fact, she argues, globalization in its current form hurts developing nations. For example, large factories built by multinational corporations consume water that local people need to drink, Rajiva maintains. Moreover, she claims, the governments of developing countries protect multinational corporations at the expense of their own people. Small farmers and local businesses cannot compete with state-supported multinationals, Rajiva asserts. Rajiva, a writer, teaches English and politics at the University of Maryland and Towson University.

As you read, consider the following questions:

1. What are some of the signs of progress Rajiva observed on the road from Madras to Vellore?
2. According to the author, how have some farmers expressed their outrage at the destruction of their lives by multinationals?
3. What type of production does the author believe is the enemy of the global village?

Lila Rajiva, "The Globalized Village," *AlterNet*, November 19, 2004.

The road from Madras to my hometown Vellore in the southern part of India makes for a bumpy ride, regardless of one's choice of transportation—be it a sturdy socialist-era Ambassador car or a newer lightweight import, a crowded dirty bus or an air-conditioned taxi. There are no lanes and the traffic moves erratically and at will, as the black tar fades indistinguishably into the neighboring sand and thorn bushes.

One side of the road has been dug up as part of the preliminary work for the Golden Quadrilateral. Hundred-year-old trees have been cut down to make way for this ambitious national highway that is expected to span the length and breadth of the country. My mother claims that this summer feels a lot hotter thanks to the ceaseless construction. But to what avail this additional three degrees of boiling heat in July when the monsoon fails? Nobody pays attention to the two lanes we have now; why should they care about getting four more?

Signs of "Progress"

Another sign of "progress" along the way is the Hyundai factory. It is one of the many gleaming new buildings—including medical colleges catering to non-resident Indians (Indians who have emigrated outside their country)—dotting the road in this part of the country. Globalization is alive and well in the villages of India.

The meals on the trains used to be served in moistened banana leaves that were plucked in front of you and thrown away after; today they are wrapped in tin foil or come in plastic or cardboard containers like the cheerfully colored juice packs. The Suzuki-owned Marutis [an Indian-made automobile] have been joined by a wide array of foreign makes. I read of high-flying elite and their Porsches and Mercedes Benz—although why anyone would risk taking them out on an Indian road is hard to imagine. I see the plastic knives and forks and cloth napkins in a small town restaurant, internet access in little shops and booths everywhere you go, a small but well stocked air-conditioned supermarket with shopping carts, bored store girls and wide empty aisles.

For a foreign-returned Indian, these symbols of "progress" soothe one's guilt for leaving behind the millions who live an attenuated existence in these paddy fields, huts and impoverished villages. It makes us feel that, finally, the world is getting better thanks to technology and capitalism. The campesino and the conglomerate are working hand in hand as the free market triumphs again.

A Darker Picture

But the gaudy veneer of liberalization is wafer-thin. Lurking beneath is a darker picture, easily visible to anyone who truly wants to see.

Let's take the Hyundai factory as an example. Ever since it opened for business, water has been in short supply for miles around. The locals don't have the water to drink, cook or bathe. In the scorching heat, this shortage is not an inconvenience but a death sentence. [In 2003] the death toll from an unexpectedly hot dry summer reached the thousands.

How does globalization feel when you have to walk a mile to the well with a squalling infant tugging at your sari and nothing to cover your head from the ferocious sun except a thin piece of old cotton? The Hyundai factory guzzles water, electricity and land. But it's good to have something more than the trundling old Ambassadors to drive around. People tell me it's a fine place to work. And won't it be splendid to see the Hyundais zip up and down the Golden Quadrilateral when it's completed.

Jobs, transportation and industry are what globalization brings with it for some, but who stands by to measure the immense fallout borne by everyone else? The collateral damage of multinational companies cannot compete with the devastation inflicted by war. Cancun can't compete with Iraq [where unrest continues after a 2003 war] for the media's attention.[1] But is death from dehydration any less painful than being killed by a bullet?

In the state of Karnataka, small farmers like the campesinos at Cancun have committed ritual suicide to express their outrage at the destruction of their lives by multinationals. They are the immediate and dramatic victims of global-

1. In September 2003 at a World Trade Organization (WTO) meeting in Cancun, Mexico, fourteen thousand farmers and indigenous people from developing nations around the world came to protest conditions they face under the WTO. Kyung Hae Lee, a fifty-six-year-old rice farmer from South Korea, stabbed himself.

Deutsch. © by Barry Deutsch. Reproduced by permission.

ization but the damage is far more widespread if less visible. Some indigenous medicines and herbs used for centuries are now in the danger of becoming the exclusive property of corporations eager to patent them.

A Battle for Intellectual Property Rights

A recent case involved turmeric, the yellow spice used to color rice and other foods in India. In 1995, two expatriate Indians at the University of Mississippi Medical Center, Suman Das and HariHar Cohly, applied for a patent for the use of turmeric as a salve for wounds—an age-old Indian remedy. The Indian Council for Scientific and Industrial Research promptly challenged the patent, even producing an article written in 1953 in the *Journal of the Indian Medical Association* that quoted ancient Sanskrit texts that referred to such use. The patent was eventually withdrawn. But nine other such patents on turmeric have since been filed. Patents have also been granted for specific uses of other indigenous products like basmati rice and neem leaves.

Intellectual property rights are at the core of the World

Trade Organization debate between the developed and underdeveloped countries. American trade lawyers argue that since patent laws are not frequently used in poorer countries, their governments do not understand them. They claim that only new applications of traditional foods and herbs are being patented, not pre-existing practices. They argue that without patent protection, drug companies have little incentive to undertake long-term and expensive research.

Hidden behind the rhetoric of the free market is a demand for the state to protect the corporation and grant it monopoly rights. And contrary to the rhetoric of the competitive market, it is the biggest companies—such as the pharmaceutical megacorporations with their wealthy executives and fat profit margins—that will profit most from this type of state protection. Meanwhile, millions of children are deprived of the simple vitamins that could save them from disease and death. If the market really worked as it should, freely, the campesinos would win much more frequently than they do now.

A Humane Globalization

But to frame the debate as one between campesino and conglomerate, between the countryside and commerce is to have already lost the war. For capital-G Globalization—like Modernity, Science, Progress, or any other capitalized abstraction—casts itself as irresistible and irreversible. Only Luddites, medievalists, agrarian romantics and the Birkenstock brigade are foolish enough to stand in its way. These are the straw men created by corporate apologists in order to dismiss the anti-globalization movement as irrational or adolescent.

We need new ways of speaking. Modernity is not the enemy. It is the relentless nature of a certain type of economic production, which is propagandized and supported by the state. Without agricultural subsidies, the big farmers would be out of business, beaten out by the small farmers. The conglomerates would be routed by the campesinos.

The resistance to multinationals is not a resistance to globalization. It is a demand to retain the perspective of the village, the perspective of all that is human. What we need today are activists *for* globalization—but a humane globalization, not an inhuman one.

VIEWPOINT

"Economic globalization and its institutions . . . have increased global poverty."

Globalization Increases Poverty in Developing Nations

Antonia Juhasz

According to Antonia Juhasz in the following viewpoint, free trade, deregulation, and financial liberalization—the policies of economic globalization—concentrate wealth in the hands of the corporate elite, drastically increasing the gap between the rich and poor both between and within countries. These policies do not alleviate poverty in developing nations; they protect multinationals and remove from local governments the tools they need to close the income gap. Juhasz is project director of the International Forum on Globalization, an organization of scholars and activists who examine the impact of globalization.

As you read, consider the following questions:

1. What warnings does the Central Intelligence Agency provide concerning economic globalization?
2. In Juhasz's opinion, why is the Bush administration making loans to Pakistan and Indonesia rather than providing direct aid?
3. Who in the U.S. population has experienced large wealth gains since 1983, in the author's view?

United States Trade Representative Robert Zoellick has begun to use the [terrorist attacks] of September 11, 2001 as a rationale to push an aggressive free trade agenda, arguing that we must "counter terrorism with trade." An expansive economic globalization agenda is one of the four policy priorities President [George W.] Bush asked Congress to address immediately following the attacks of September 11. The administration is arguing that we will end terrorism through trade because economic globalization is the solution to poverty. But all evidence shows the contrary, that economic globalization is a cause of global poverty and inequality, not a solution. Furthermore, this evidence is increasingly coming from within the institutions of economic globalization itself.

Increasing Global Poverty

For example, the Central Intelligence Agency itself warned in a December 2000 report that economic globalization would increase inequality and poverty, thereby fostering violence: "The rising tide of the global economy will create many economic winners, but it will not lift all boats. . . . [It will] spawn conflicts at home and abroad, ensuring an even wider gap between regional winners and losers than exists today. . . . [Globalization's] evolution will be rocky, marked by chronic financial volatility and a widening economic divide. Regions, countries, and groups feeling left behind will face deepening economic stagnation, political instability, and cultural alienation. *They will foster political, ethnic, ideological, and religious extremism, along with the violence that often accompanies it* [emphasis added]."

The most reliable data available, predominantly from *supporters* of economic globalization, demonstrate how economic globalization has caused the most dramatic increase in global inequality and poverty in modern history. Furthermore, this outcome is intrinsic to the economic globalization model. Arguments that economic globalization allows "fragile democracies" to "overcome poverty and create opportunity," as Trade Representative Zoellick wrote in the *Washington Post*, are seriously mistaken. If such policies are pursued, the world could find itself in even worse circumstances in the future than those we find ourselves in today.

The administration has already begun to move ahead with IMF [International Monetary Fund] loans to Pakistan and Indonesia in the name of fighting terrorism. If we wish to help these countries with their economic problems, why are we providing loans instead of direct aid? Why are we using the IMF, an institution that has failed miserably in this region (as former World Bank chief economist Joseph Stiglitz wrote, "All the IMF did was make East Asia's recessions deeper, longer, and harder.") instead of alternative funding sources, such as the United Nations, that historically represent the interests of developing countries? The answer may be that the U.S. government can control the funds that go to a country through the IMF by linking conditions to the loans. These conditions have historically benefited corporate and elite interests over those of the populations of the countries in question.

Marginalizing the Poor

The CIA is not alone in its assessment of the catastrophic impact that the policies of economic globalization have had around the world. For example, the World Bank—one of economic globalization's leading institutions—reports that "Globalization appears to increase poverty and inequality. . . . The costs of adjusting to greater openness are borne exclusively by the poor, regardless of how long the adjustment takes."

The United Nations echoes these words in its 1999 Human Development Report, "The new rules of globalization—and the players writing them—focus on integrating global markets, neglecting the needs of people that markets cannot meet. The process is concentrating power and marginalizing the poor, both countries and people. . . . The current [globalization] debate is . . . too narrow . . . neglecting broader human concerns such as persistent global poverty, growing inequality between and within countries, exclusion of poor people and countries and persistent human rights abuses."

The policies of economic globalization such as free trade, financial liberalization, deregulation, reduced government spending, and privatization concentrate wealth at the top, removing from governments and communities the very tools

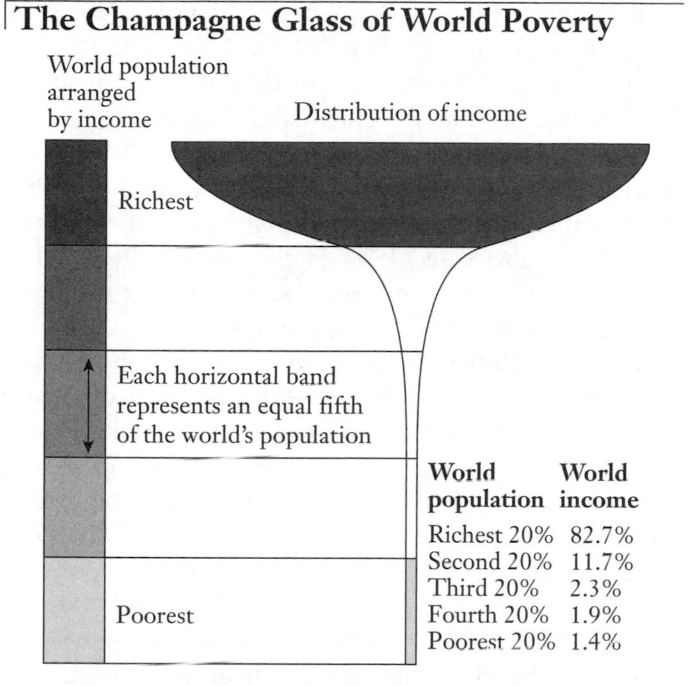

United Nations Development Programme, Human Development Report, 1992.

needed to ensure equity and to protect workers, social services, the environment, and sustainable livelihoods. In this way, economic globalization and its institutions—including the International Monetary Fund (IMF), the World Bank, the World Trade Organization, and the North American Free Trade Agreement—have created the most dramatic increase in global inequality—both within and between nations—in modern history and have increased global poverty.

The Income Gap

For example, the income gap between the fifth of the world's people living in the richest countries and the fifth in the poorest doubled from 1960 to 1990, from thirty to one to sixty to one. By 1998 it had jumped again, with the gap widening to an astonishing seventy-eight to one. Poverty trends have worsened as well; there are 100 million more poor people in developing countries today than a decade ago. The assets of the three richest people on earth are greater than the combined Gross National Product of the forty-eight least developed countries. Even in the United States, where median earnings of workers more than doubled from 1947 and 1973, the past two decades have seen median earnings fall by almost 15 percent, with the earnings for the poorest 20 percent of households falling the furthest behind. In fact, the only segment of the U.S. population that has experienced large wealth gains since 1983 is the richest 20 percent of households. The net worth of the top 1 percent of U.S. households now exceeds that of the bottom 90 percent.

As Professor Robert Wade of the London School of Economics wrote in *The Economist*, "Global inequality is worsening rapidly. . . . Technological change and financial liberalization result in a disproportionately fast increase in the number of households at the extreme rich end, without shrinking the distribution at the poor end. . . . From 1988 to 1993, the share of the world income going to the poorest 10 percent of the world's population fell by over a quarter, whereas the share of the richest 10 percent rose by 8 percent. The richest 10 percent pulled away from the median, while the poorest 10 percent fell away from the median, falling absolutely and by a large amount."

It is time to recognize that economic globalization does not serve the poor, it serves the wealthy. It actually adds to the numbers of poor while concentrating greater amounts of wealth among an ever-dwindling number of people. As Thabo Mbeki, the president of South Africa, said, "We believe consciousness is rising, including in the North, about the inequality and insecurity globalization has brought about the plight of poor countries." For the U.S. Trade Representative to argue that expanding the World Trade Organization, signing the Free Trade Area of the Americas, and granting the President "Trade Promotion Authority" (formally Fast Track) to side-step Congress in the creation of national legislation will address the root problems of global instability is opportunistic, disrespectful, and cynical. It is time to reject failed models and embrace new alternatives.

"Those poor nations [that] join the globalization revolution are the very ones now prospering."

Globalization Reduces Poverty in Developing Nations

Jim Peron

Poverty is decreasing in developing nations that have embraced the most recent wave of globalization, argues Jim Peron in the following viewpoint. Peron maintains that in the 1980s developing nations that eliminated trade barriers began to benefit from globalization. Studies of globalization's impact during this period show a reduction in global income inequality and an increase in living standards, he contends. Peron is executive director of the Institute for Liberal Values, a think tank that opposes big government.

As you read, consider the following questions:

1. According to Peron, why must studies of wealth inequality look at more than income alone?
2. What is the result of having studies that use different standards of "absolute poverty," in the author's view?
3. In the author's opinion, what could be hidden by a substantial increase in world population?

Jim Peron, "World Inequality and Globalization," *Scoop*, August 18, 2002.

World inequality is increasing. That's one of the major claims of Greens, Reds[1] and assorted anti-globalization "activists." Take Grassroots International as just one example. They have claimed: "Inequality, by any definition, has increased."

Not only that but: "The rich have become much richer as the ranks of the very poor have swelled dramatically and their living conditions have deteriorated."

Well that's a challenge if I ever saw one. More importantly it's a blatant falsehood. But if one is going to trash globalization the best way to do this is by manufacturing phony claims like this one.

Examining the Claims

First we should look at the idea that "inequality, by any definition, has increased." Xavier Sala-i-Martin is one of the most cited economists in the world today. And his investigation of "The Disturbing 'Rise' of Global Income Inequality" shows that inequality has lessened not increased.

Professor Sala-i-Martin used seven major indexes which measure inequality. Applying them across the globe for the period 1980 to 1998—which is when the last wave of globalization took place—he finds that: "All indexes show a reduction in global income inequality between 1980 and 1998." By all seven methods inequality was reduced. Yet the anti-globalizers say that by "any definition" it has increased. Obviously they were wrong.

But what about the claim that, "the very poor have swelled dramatically and their living conditions have deteriorated"? That too is a falsehood. The good Professor notes that "There are between 300 and 500 million less poor people in 1998 than there were in the 70s."

Prof. Sala-i-Martin is not alone. The United Nations Development Programme decided to see what the trend was in wealth inequality as well. But you can't simply look at income since $1 in Lusaka buys a lot more goods than $1 does in

1. The term *Greens* often refers to members of the Green Party, which supports policies that protect the environment and human rights. Reds are those who oppose capitalism and support Communist economic policies.

London. So they compared the purchasing power of the richest 20% of the world population to the 20% of the population with the least money. They covered the period from 1970 to 1998 and found "the ratio fell, from 15 to 1 to 13 to 1." In other words world income had become more equal.

The Causes of Global Poverty

"Globalization" has become a lightning rod for many legitimate concerns about modern society including poverty, inequality, unemployment, and environmental degradation. Yet, there is no clear evidence that globalization per se is to blame for rising global poverty or inequality. Indeed, higher levels of trade and investment tend to increase economic growth and bring other positive spillover effects (such as access to new, better technologies). Rather than blanket claims against globalization, there emerges a pattern in which some countries successfully reap the benefits of the global economy while others are being left behind. Those that fall behind (such as sub-Saharan Africa) fail on a range of indicators. The causes of their marginalization are more deep-seated and complex than simply globalization and include factors such as a lack of investment, poor education, weak infrastructure and institutions, and civil and political unrest.

Jenny Bates, *Policy Report*, August 29, 2000.

They also found that instead of worsening, living conditions for the world's poor have improved substantially. "Many more people can enjoy a decent standard of living, with average incomes in developing countries having almost doubled in real terms between 1975 and 1998 . . . "

Inflating the Numbers

A standard for "absolute poverty" was established at $1 per day (using 1985 dollars) by the World Bank. Professor Sala-i-Martin was a bit perplexed to find that official poverty organizations have been adjusting the number. "For some reason, another poverty line mysteriously appeared in the literature that doubled the original figure to two dollars per day. The United Nations sometimes uses four dollars per day."

This leads to an artificial inflation of the numbers of people in absolute poverty. "Of course, if one is allowed to raise the poverty line arbitrarily, then one is bound to find all persons in the world are poor." Using the $1 per day and $2 per day numbers Sala-i-Martin still found a decrease in the number of those suffering absolute poverty. "The $1/day poverty rate has fallen from 20% to 5% over the last twenty five years. The $2/day rate has fallen from 44% to 18%."

This good news could be misleading since a smaller percentage of poor people in a larger population can still translate into more poor people in total. And since the world population has increased substantially a percentage decline in poverty could well hide a rise in the total number of poor. But in this case the good news remains true. "We see that, using the one-dollar-a-day definition, the overall number of poor declined by over 400 million people: from close to 700 million citizens in the peak year of 1974, to less than 300 million in 1998. Using the two-dollar definition the number of poor declined by about 500 million: from 1.48 billion to 980 million in 1998."

The Benefits of Participating in Global Trade

Now let's go back to the anti-globalization crusaders we discussed in the first paragraph. They are claiming that poverty and inequality have increased as a result of globalization. Yet it is precisely during the period of greatest globalization that poverty and inequality have diminished.

Previous waves of globalization didn't help the poor of the world in general. In fact poverty and inequality continued to increase until the most recent globalization wave. What changed? From the late 1800s to World War I free trade and globalization was restricted to mainly Western nations. They saw increased prosperity but the poor nations weren't part of that trade. After the War trade protectionism ruled and poverty and inequality, as to be expected, increased. Trade nationalism made world wealth even less equal.

Only in the recent wave of globalization have the poor nations of the world participated. Beginning around 1980 many Third World nations started lowering tariffs and deregulating. Today we have two Third Worlds. The first joined the globalization revolution and are seeing growth rates averaging 5% per annum. This means they are rapidly catching up with the wealthy nations of the world which are growing at only 2% per year. And those Third World nations that are practicing economic nationalism are uniformly regressing.

The anti-globalizers have everything almost perfectly backwards. World-wide poverty is decreasing not increasing. Inequality is waning not rising. And those poor nations which join the globalization revolution are the very ones now prospering. Those who listen to the anti-globalizers are wallowing in poverty and misery with little hope of getting out.

VIEWPOINT 5

"For countries that have endured decades of severe indebtedness, . . . cancellation of their outstanding debt, without externally imposed conditions, is necessary."

Canceling Debts to Global Financial Institutions Will Help Developing Nations

Soren Ambrose

Forcing developing nations to pay enormous debts to international financial institutions created to promote globalization keeps these nations in poverty, argues Soren Ambrose in the following viewpoint. Moreover, debt-relief policies that require developing nations to participate in globalization by opening up their economies benefits multinational corporations, not the nations' people, Ambrose claims. When developing nations spend huge sums servicing their debts, social programs and local producers suffer, he asserts. Ambrose is a policy analyst with 50 Years is Enough, a coalition committed to reforming international financial policy.

As you read, consider the following questions:

1. According to Ambrose, what special incentive do borrowing governments have to stay current with their multilateral debts?
2. In the author's opinion, why can the United States veto policy decisions of the World Bank and International Monetary Fund?
3. How would the status of international financial institutions change under a system of impartial international debt arbitration, in the author's view?

Soren Ambrose, "Multilateral Debt: The Unbearable Burden," *Foreign Policy in Focus*, vol. 6, November 2001.

Multilateral debt is that portion of a country's external debt burden owed to international financial institutions (IFIs) such as the International Monetary Fund (IMF) and the World Bank. For most of the world's impoverished countries, multilateral debt looms larger than other debts because of the status of IFIs as "preferred creditors" assigned them by the Group of 7 (G-7)[1] industrialized countries. These same countries control the most votes at the IFIs and use the resulting leverage to insist on orthodox austerity and "free trade" policies. Because of the preferred creditor status of the IFIs, payments of multilateral debt takes priority over private and bilateral (government-to-government) debt.

The Multilateral Debt Crisis

Governments and private creditors often write off debts. But the IFIs contend that their bylaws prohibit them from granting debt relief or canceling debts. Borrowing governments have special incentive to stay current with their multilateral debts because IFIs determine the creditworthiness of borrowing countries. Until the IMF gives its stamp of approval that a country is adhering to the economic policies it recommends, impoverished countries generally cannot get credit or capital from other sources. Until a country has signed onto an IMF program, it cannot apply for bilateral debt relief from the "Paris Club"[2] of creditor countries.

The significant growth of multilateral debt came to public attention with the Latin American debt crisis of the early 1980s. Mexico, Argentina, and Brazil all came to the brink of defaulting on loans that foreign banking corporations had freely offered to developing country governments during the 1970s. The IMF and the World Bank responded with massive loan packages conditioned on implementation of structural adjustment programs (SAPs), which are packages of neoliberal economic policy reforms ostensibly designed to

1. The G-7 includes the United States, Japan, Germany, France, the United Kingdom, Italy, and Canada. The G-7 became the G-8 in 1998 with the inclusion of Russia. 2. Comprised of financial leaders from nineteen of the world's wealthiest nations, the "Paris Club" considers appeals from countries whose debt quagmires may stem from military conflict or brutal dictatorship. These debtors are often recommended by the IMF after having tried austerity plans and other reforms. A Paris Club debt rescheduling or debt cancellation is often viewed as a last resort before default.

restore economic health to indebted countries. This promotion of SAPs marked a changing course at both IFIs. The IMF shifted from short-term, balance-of-payment loans, mainly to industrialized countries, to medium-term loans for developing nations. The World Bank added policy-linked loans to its infrastructure development projects. Private debts were converted into multilateral debt as countries used the funds acquired from the IFIs to pay off the private banks that refused to issue new loans.

The Impact of Multilateral Debt

Multilateral debt is a problem for the entire Global South,[3] but it's particularly acute for the most impoverished countries. For low-income countries (defined by the World Bank as those with per capita GNP below $785), multilateral debt increased by some 544% between 1980 and 1997, from $24.1 billion to $155.3 billion. Multilateral debt constitutes 32.75% of the long-term debt burden of the most impoverished countries. For middle-income countries, the corresponding percentage is 15%. World Bank figures for 1999 show that on average $128 million is transferred every day from the 62 most impoverished countries to wealthy countries, and that for every dollar these countries receive in grant aid, they repay $13 on old debts.

The debilitating impact of debt is felt in two main ways: 1) through the diversion of national resources to debt servicing, and 2) through the negative social and economic consequences of the SAPs that indebted countries are obligated to adopt. These SAPs are designed to transform economies from a focus on production for the local market to one that adopts a "globalized" model of production and export of products that earn the most hard currency. SAP-linked IFI loans are meant to finance the redesign of governmental, industrial, and commercial systems that will enable countries to service debts and become more integrated into the global economy. However, SAPs have almost invariably caused increased poverty, unemployment, and environmental destruction, while also leading to an increase in the overall size

3. The majority of developing nations are located in the Southern Hemisphere.

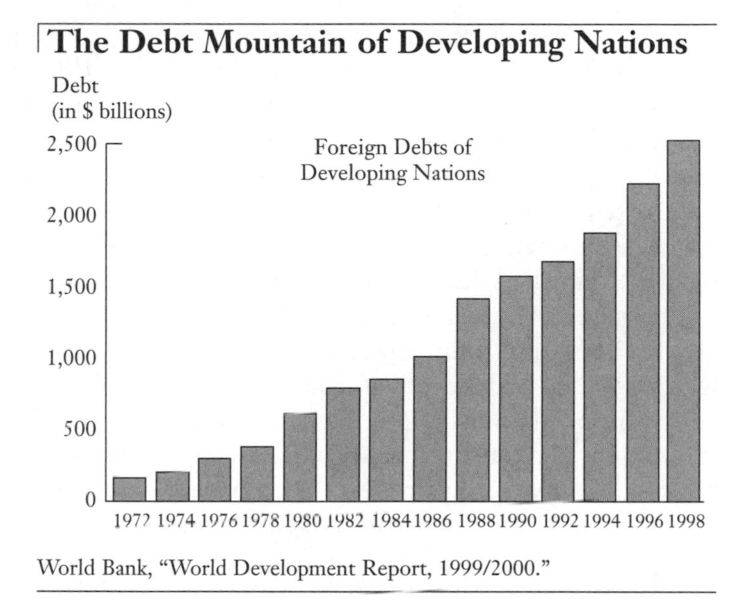

The Debt Mountain of Developing Nations

World Bank, "World Development Report, 1999/2000."

of a country's multilateral debt. The universal failure of the standard SAP recipe has meant that debt and structural adjustment simply end up fueling each other.

Looking for Solutions

The global Jubilee 2000 debt-cancellation movement, which acquired great momentum in some 50 countries in the late 1990s, has continued under different names since 2000. The latest version of the IMF/World Bank debt management program, sometimes called the Cologne initiative (after the site of the 1999 summit of the G-7 countries), was a response, however inadequate, to the Jubilee movement. As part of the Cologne terms, the U.S. and other G-7 governments agreed to cancel 100% of the bilateral debts owed them by the most impoverished countries—as long as they are obeying structural adjustment programs. Despite the high hopes of many debt-cancellation campaigners, the G-7 Summit in Genoa in 2001 yielded no new decisions or initiatives on debt. . . .

The Problems with Current U.S. Policy

Voting power at the World Bank and the IMF is apportioned according to the size of each country's monetary contribution. The U.S. has by far the largest share (18% of all votes) and can veto policy decisions, since they require an 85% vote. *The New York Times* has gone so far as to describe the IMF as a "proxy" of the U.S. government. Any analysis of IFI policies is thus also a critique of U.S. policies.

The value of the leverage associated with multilateral debt and the extent to which the G-7 controls the IFIs are evident at times of international crisis. Just as Egyptian and Kenyan debts were cancelled during the Gulf War, so in the wake of the September 11 [2001 terrorist] attacks Pakistan was induced to assist the fight against [the terrorist group] al-Qaeda and the Taliban [the former fundamental Islamist government of Afghanistan] with promises of debt cancellation, and new loans from the IMF. Should the crisis persist, Indonesia, with one of the largest debt burdens as well as the largest Muslim population, will likely benefit as well.

The Heavily Indebted Poor Countries Initiative

The main response of the World Bank and the IMF to the impoverished countries' debt crisis has been the Heavily Indebted Poor Countries (HIPC) Initiative of 1996. The ostensible aim of the program is to make the debt burden of the poorest and most indebted countries "sustainable." Once a country is deemed eligible, it must demonstrate a commitment to "sound economic policies"—the IFIs' usual euphemism for SAPs—to receive debt relief.

Under the original HIPC program, a country could not obtain benefits until it completed a second 3-year SAP. In contrast, the 1999 Cologne terms allow for some debt servicing to be suspended upon completion of the first SAP, though the original servicing terms apparently can be reinstated if the second SAP is not implemented to the IMF's satisfaction. For countries in desperate need of debt relief so they can begin to direct resources to social sectors, this type of provisional debt relief is a cruel paradox. To obtain relief, debtor nations are first required to demonstrate their willingness to make socioeconomic—and perhaps political—conditions worse by adopting programs that starve people of health care, food subsidies, and education.

HIPC's curious goal of "debt sustainability" basically refers to an assessment of the debt servicing a country can afford without going completely broke. The indicator—a debt-to-export ratio of 150%—was, as the IFIs admit, chosen arbitrarily. The unsustainability of the IFIs' approach to debt reduction was amply illustrated by the case of Uganda, the first country to go through the HIPC process. Less than a year after being accorded its debt relief, Uganda's economic indicators had slipped, due to a fall in the price of coffee, to the point where it qualified for HIPC again. (It has, in fact, received a second set of benefits under the Cologne initiative.) Seven additional countries are projected to lapse into debt-servicing unsustainability after HIPC. Two countries, Zambia and Niger, face the prospect of higher debt service costs after HIPC, thanks to the program's complex and counterproductive formulas of sustainability.

The first 22 countries to qualify for HIPC are still spending more on debt servicing than on health care. For those that have begun to get relief as of the end of 2000, the average overall reduction amounts to 27%—not a trivial decrease but hardly the kind of sweeping cancellation needed to transform economies and to make them sustainable. These qualifying debtor countries continue to spend $1.3 billion a year on debt service.

Preserving Control

The new version of HIPC seeks to ensure that debt relief will effectively reduce poverty through the Poverty Reduction Strategy Paper (PRSP), through which governments and civil society ostensibly design their budget and economic program together. But in the first countries to formulate PRSPs, macroeconomic policy emerged from discussions between governments and the IFIs without any meaningful civil society participation. Restricting civil society input to narrow budgeting discussions and to efforts to gauge poverty levels ensures that the PRSP will continue to be an instrument of the standard policies of structural adjustment: high interest rates, trade and investment liberalization, privatization, elimination of subsidies, cuts in public sector jobs and social programs. Now, limited participation of civil society risks giving the SAPs the appearance of enjoying popular approval.

The meager results of the HIPC program suggest that its promises are hollow ones, made solely to ensure that countries remain on the debt-and-structural-adjustment treadmill. Otherwise, these countries might be tempted to default or opt out of the global financial system altogether, despite the prospect of losing access to markets and capital. The IFIs and the U.S. government also have incentives to avert defaults: any gaps in the globalized economy represent reduced control and loss of potential markets. A delinking through debt default may even present an attractive alternative model for economic development independent of U.S. influence.

Preservation of that influence and control is a far more important factor in the U.S. approach to debt policy than recovery of the funds loaned. Illustrating this point was U.S. policy in the wake of Hurricane Mitch's devastation in Central America in 1998. Treasury Department officials privately gave "loss of leverage" as their reason for refusing to consider comprehensive debt cancellation for Nicaragua and Honduras. . . .

Toward a New Foreign Policy

For countries that have endured decades of severe indebtedness, poverty, and subordination to the IFIs' economic policies, comprehensive cancellation of their outstanding debt, without externally imposed conditions, is necessary if their people are ever to gain democratic control of their economic destiny. As part of that cancellation, there should be a reckoning with the question of the legitimacy of much of the current debt.

The U.S. government should ideally take the lead in such a program of cancellation, first by canceling the bilateral debt of the most impoverished countries without creditor-imposed conditions, and then strongly urging similar cancellation of multilateral debt. It should also advocate for and participate in a "truth commission" on the accumulation and abuse of debt over the years, as a way of establishing the legitimacy or illegitimacy of debts that national populations have been asked to pay. That process could be linked to a new system in which an international arbitration court arbitrates debt disputes and arrears independent of the IFIs.

Such a system would address both countries on the "debt treadmill" and countries with currency crises. Instead of a drawn-out drama like the one Argentina has endured since 1998, culminating in a virtual default in late 2001 despite three IMF "bailout" packages, a country in crisis could submit to the insolvency procedures of an independent court and begin to re-establish its productivity with a minimum of damage to the more vulnerable parts of the population.

An International Court

University of Vienna economist Kunibert Raffer has suggested a process for recognizing partial insolvency of national governments. Raffer cites provisions in U.S. law permitting debts of local governments to be treated like those of a company or an individual who has gone bankrupt, while guaranteeing that essential services provided by the municipality are not affected. His recommendation is echoed by a November 2001 report issued by an "emerging markets eminent persons group" of widely respected former finance ministers of South Korea, India, and Ghana, and the former head of Chile's central bank. Although Raffer maintains that this process could occur without the creation of a new international agency—he suggests a panel of arbitrators with equal creditor/debtor representation—it is hard to imagine that the World Bank and the IMF would have adequate incentive to participate without the creation of some new regimen. This would require that the United Nations or World Court establish a body with authority over the IFIs and both creditor and debtor governments.

Once constituted, the new international court of arbitration would function much like courts in the U.S. adjudicating cases of insolvency or bankruptcy. It would be empowered to instruct creditors to accept a portion of their claims and demand no more, and it would establish a process for cleansing a country's credit record, so that nation could reenter the global economy on fair terms. This new court would not have the power to insist on particular economic programs as a condition for debt reduction.

The IFIs and some powerful governments would likely object to such a debt arbitration system on the grounds that the IFIs' status as preferred creditors would be threatened if decisions on debt relief were removed from their control. Such concerns should be met with the insistence that the IFIs must take some responsibility for the effects of the policies they have imposed around the world. In a similar vein, the World Bank should be pressured to annul debts owed to it for projects its own analyses show to be economic failures. (A 1992 World Bank report, Effective Implementation, estimated 37.5% of World Bank projects should be so classified.) The proposed court should perform an assessment of which IFI claims are legitimate in light of their poor policy advice and failed projects.

The IFIs should also be forced to accept—through a change in their bylaws, if necessary—the option of writing off debts. Private banks do this routinely with loans they can never expect to be repaid, and many took some losses in resolving the Latin American debt crisis in the early 1980s. The current HIPC program does not mandate that the IFIs write off debt; instead they simply agree to accept full payment of the debts from a fund created by donations from wealthier governments.

Activists in Jubilee South, which brings together debt cancellation campaigns from across Latin America, the Caribbean, Asia-Pacific, and Africa, emphasize the imperative of assessing "who owes whom:" after the exploitation of slavery, colonialism, and the current economic system, their insistence that Southern governments should repudiate their debts, and that Northern governments and institutions should pay reparations and restitution cannot be lightly dismissed as too radical or too unrealistic. At this point, realizing economic and moral justice would require a deeper accounting of past practices than most governments and institutions are prepared to make.

Viewpoint 6

"Total cancellation [of debts] would seriously jeopardize the overall flow of financial support for the poorest countries."

Canceling Debts to Global Financial Institutions Will Hurt Developing Nations

International Monetary Fund and World Bank

The International Monetary Fund (IMF) and the World Bank are international financial institutions created to promote globalization by lending money to developing nations that open up their economies to global trade. In the following viewpoint the institutions contend that canceling all debts owed to international lending institutions would hurt developing nations. Total debt cancellation would jeopardize the ability of these institutions to continue providing financial support to developing nations that have demonstrated their commitment to globalization, the authors claim. Moreover, loans to nations committed to peace and global trade will be more effective at reducing global poverty than would total debt cancellation, they argue.

As you read, consider the following questions:

1. In the opinion of the IMF and the World Bank, what are some of the many factors that contribute to poverty in developing countries?
2. What evidence do the authors cite proving that the HIPC Initiative is relieving poverty?

International Monetary Fund and World Bank Staffs, "100 Percent Debt Cancellation? A Response from the IMF and the World Bank," www.imf.org, July 10, 2001.

At the close of the last millennium, the international community succeeded in achieving an ambitious and important goal in our shared fight against poverty. In 1999, we committed ourselves to "deeper, broader and faster" debt relief to every eligible country which could translate the resources into better prospects for its poor. By the end of June 2001, agreements were in place—with relief flowing—to 23 countries, 19 of them in Africa, for debt service relief amounting to some $34 billion. And we are committed to helping the remaining HIPCs [Heavily Indebted Poor Countries] do what is necessary to access debt relief under the Initiative.

The progress to date is a crucial step in the fight against poverty, but much more needs to be done. The deep concerns of civil society in many countries helped to spur the international community to action in the HIPC Initiative. Now some debt relief campaigners are calling for a complete cancellation of all HIPC debts. Some are focusing their efforts on the international financial institutions. Is this really the best way to ensure that resources are available to attack poverty and promote development in the low-income countries?

This [viewpoint] considers the implications of proposals to cancel 100 percent of multilateral debt. First, it sets debt relief in the context of a broad strategy to fight poverty. Second it looks at the existing approach to poor country debt relief through the HIPC Initiative. Third, it turns to the fundamental question of what would be gained by such a proposal. Finally, the implications for development finance are looked at, including who would end up paying.

The Strategy for Reducing Poverty

Many factors contribute to poverty in developing countries: economic and political history, poor economic management, weak governance, armed conflict and such external factors as deteriorating terms of trade and climatic problems. In about half of the 80 poorest countries, unsustainably high external debt has also become a key constraint on development.

Reducing world poverty is today's central development challenge. To do this we need to follow through on a comprehensive strategy to reduce poverty, based on the twin pillars of home-grown efforts by all the HIPCs to create the basis for sustained pro-poor growth, and on more decisive support from the international community.

Africa's leaders have reaffirmed their countries' responsibility to address the local obstacles to poverty alleviation. They recognize the importance of sustaining reform to avoid unsustainable debt burdens, and to restore investor confidence. Their efforts should focus on implementing national poverty reduction and growth strategies. This means creating delivery capacity for social policy, better expenditure management, and the many other elements of economic, social, political and institutional reform. For its part, the international community must respond by providing more official development assistance on appropriate terms, opening markets for poor countries, assisting with building capacity, and providing well-targeted debt relief.

The HIPC Initiative should be seen as part of this comprehensive approach. It is removing debt as a constraint in poor countries' struggle against poverty. It sets the stage for determined countries, supported by the international community, to overcome other constraints to exiting from poverty.

The Heavily Indebted Poor Countries Initiative

The agreements in place for the 23 countries mentioned above, with other sources of debt relief, reduce their total debt by two-thirds, bringing their indebtedness to levels below the average for all developing countries. Cash debt service savings in these countries are also substantial—about US$1.1 billion annually in the next three years. Debt service payments as a percentage of exports, GDP [gross domestic product] and government revenues will fall dramatically.

This is real progress. One important reason the Initiative is working is that, for the first time, debt relief is delivered within a framework that is transparent and comprehensive, and that, crucially, provides for equitable participation by all parties. Also unique, is that relief is delivered only to those countries which have demonstrated the commitment and capacity to use the resources effectively. These principles reflect the fact that debt relief comes at a cost. In a world of scarce development resources it is crucial to ensure that debt relief will actually make a difference in the lives of the poor.

These countries have been receiving an average of about $10 billion per year in grants and concessional loans. After HIPC debt relief is taken into account, their debt service obligations will fall to less than $2 billion per year (of which 10 percent is owed to the World Bank and 12 percent to IMF [International Monetary Fund]). In addition, a number of creditor governments have recently signaled their intention to provide additional debt reduction beyond the HIPC Initiative. These are welcome initiatives, although it is essential that the relief is not offset by reductions in aid flows. The figures above illustrate the importance of maintaining new flows of assistance if debt relief is to add to poverty reduction efforts: a decline of just 10 percent in new flows would wipe out the benefits of HIPC debt relief, and a total cancellation of debt would be offset by a cut of 20 percent in aid flows. Since total debt cancellation would require concerted action by all creditors, many of which continue to provide assistance, total cancellation would seriously jeopardize the overall flow of financial support for the poorest countries.

The Argument for Total Debt Relief

What is the argument for total debt cancellation? Some argue that the further reduction of debt service obligations would allow the HIPCs to make more poverty-related investments. But the HIPC Initiative is already changing the picture. So far, after debt relief, social expenditures in the 23 HIPCs mentioned above are projected to rise by an average of some US$1.7 billion per year during 2001–2002. Most of these resources will be directed toward health, education, HIV/AIDS programs, basic infrastructure and governance reform. And contrary to the statements of some debt campaigners, HIPCs will spend on average much more—not less—on priority social investments than on debt service. After HIPC relief, these countries will spend about 2 percent of GDP on debt service—well below the level in other developing countries—compared to about 7 percent on social expenditures.

To be sure, the HIPCs have a continuing need for targeted investment that benefits the poor. But the critical question is whether complete debt cancellation is the most effective and equitable way of supporting these efforts.

The debt reduction under the HIPC Initiative should be seen as a one-time action, the first step toward enabling the HIPCs to stand on their own feet. Their growth and poverty reduction strategies need financial support, which for many will mean a need for a much higher level of concessional official aid for many years to come. In time, they will become able to gain access to private international capital, including both direct investment and further borrowing.

Critics Caution Against Forgiveness

Opponents of complete debt forgiveness do not deny that developing countries' debt burdens need to be relieved. However, they say that the complete cancellation of debt will not help lift those countries out of poverty, and furthermore, could cause more harm than good.

Critics say that debt forgiveness will not solve the problem of poverty because it does not address the root causes of poverty —ineffective or harmful government policies. . . .

Opponents warn [that] forgiveness would actually encourage poor economic policies by teaching governments that they can squander money and not be held responsible. Furthermore, forgiveness would also reward and encourage corrupt leaders who misappropriated the loans for their own use, they argue.

Issues & Controversies, February 16, 2001.

Credit is an indispensable means of financing development, and for decades has helped developing countries become active participants in the global economy. It must, however, take place in a climate of mutual trust. It should be on appropriate terms, it should not be used to excess and must not be allowed to become unmanageable for the debtor. Equally, creditors should have confidence that loans can and will be repaid.

The Importance of Borrowing

Some object to the very concept of poor countries borrowing for their development. But borrowing remains a crucial part of external assistance. In fact, HIPCs already receive significant net transfers of assistance in the form of highly concessional loans, especially from multilateral institutions.

Most multilateral institutions, including the World Bank through IDA [International Development Agency] and the IMF through the PRGF [Poverty Reduction and Growth Facility], provide resources to poor countries through cooperative arrangements on highly concessional terms. This is a unique source of concessional finance for the world's neediest countries which operates on the principle that developing countries borrow from and pay back into the same sources of financing. The preferred creditor status of the IMF, World Bank and other international financial institutions ensures that they are able to continue to provide financial support to their members on a sustainable basis, even in very difficult circumstances.

Of course, good results from borrowing were not seen everywhere. Some countries, for many different reasons, have not experienced significant gains. In HIPCs, unsustainable debt is a result. The international community has a collective obligation to address this problem. The HIPC Initiative is doing this. But we must also be there to support the future development needs for *all* countries. That is why the goal of the Initiative is to help countries achieve debt sustainability, and is focussed specifically on the most highly indebted poor countries. Total debt cancellation for those countries alone would come at the expense of other borrowing countries, including those non-HIPCs which are home to 80 percent of the developing world's poor. Those who call for 100 percent cancellation for the HIPCs alone, must recognize that this would be inequitable for other poor countries.

Maintaining the Capacity to Finance Development

Supporters of 100 percent debt cancellation must be honest about the costs. The total public external debt for low-income countries stands at some $460 billion. HIPCs and many other poor countries will rely on external financing for their development needs long into the future. A growing portion of this need is being met by bilateral and multilateral agencies on concessional terms. Total cancellation could imperil these funds. It would also undermine the confidence of existing and potential investors whose funds are vital for the long-term development of the low-income countries.

Beyond the flows from bilateral donors, the only other concessional financing comes from multilateral agencies, primarily the multilateral development banks and the IMF. These concessional flows are financed in two main ways: (i) budget allocations by developed countries; and (ii) repayment of the concessional loans made previously by these agencies. Of course, the community of shareholders could make a special budget allocation to pay for the cost of additional debt relief or new financing by the multilateral agencies, but at present there is little support in donor countries to do so. In these circumstances, what would be the effect on these agencies of a complete cancellation of the debt owed to these institutions?

The Cost to Multilateral Agencies

IDA finances nearly half of its new commitments (about $6.5 billion annually) from repayments and investment income. As IDA has no provisions for losses arising on its credits to members, this means that write-offs would be a direct dollar-for-dollar reduction in IDA's ability to make future credits to poor countries. In effect, credits would be cut in half. Alternatively, to maintain future IDA lending at this level, contributions from the developed countries would have to double, a response which seems highly unlikely.

The regional development banks (IDB [Inter-American Development Bank], AfDB [African Development Bank], AsDB [Asian Development Bank]) also have soft lending windows, and face even greater constraints, since they are also dependent on the contributions from the developed countries. Indeed, the AfDB continues to face an uphill task in securing full financing of its share of HIPC costs under the existing arrangements. Total debt cancellation would likely cripple these institutions.

The IMF's Poverty Reduction and Growth Facility is also funded by contributions and borrowed resources. Although it is now close to being a permanent facility, its future operations will be financed purely by reflows. Debt cancellation would deplete the resources of the PRGF Trust and force closure of the facility. No resources would remain available for future concessional IMF lending, and the IMF would have to withdraw from providing concessional support to its poorest members.

But what of the nonconcessional resources of the multilaterals? The question is often asked whether the "hard" lending facilities of multilateral development banks and the IMF can pay for debt relief provided by the "soft" lending windows—beyond the substantial contributions to IDA & HIPC already being made from IBRD [International Bank for Reconstruction and Development] net income. The fact is that the hard lending windows already use their paid-in capital and reserves to underpin lending to developing country members. Provisions are taken against expected losses related to exposure on the balance sheets of multilateral development banks, and cannot be used to write off losses on other balance sheets without putting the institution at risk of going out of business.

The IBRD's equity capital is leveraged at a rate of about 5:1 through the issuance of AAA-rated debt. Therefore, its capacity to lend would be reduced by $5 for every $1 distributed to debt relief in respect of the concessional lenders' balance sheets. Furthermore, it is likely that the write-off would result in a weaker equity capital position for the Bank and therefore an increased cost of lending to its borrowers. Debt cancellation, with substantially reduced borrowing, at higher cost, would have a serious impact on IBRD-eligible borrowers, which are home to 80 percent of the world's poorest people.

The IMF: For the Fund, total debt cancellation in the absence of full funding by bilateral donors would do serious damage by fundamentally changing its role as an anchor for the international financial system based on the revolving character of its resources. Debt cancellation would not only eliminate PRGF lending, but also impair the Fund's financial integrity. The IMF's gold reserves are a fundamental strength in its financial position, giving it increased credibility and the capacity to assist its broader membership in crisis situations. The 1999 decision by the membership to use, as an exceptional one-time measure, income from the investments of the profits from limited off-market gold sales to help finance the IMF's contribution to the HIPC Initiative had a substantial cost to the institution and its members. Additional sales would put at risk the confidence of members in the Fund's solidity, and thus its ability to lend.

The Way Forward

We have made a great deal of progress in implementing the enhanced HIPC Initiative, but there is much more to do. The next challenge is to move forward with debt relief agreements for those countries which have yet to qualify for HIPC relief because of conflict or severe governance problems. With countries committed to peace and stability, we believe HIPC relief can contribute to the transition from conflict to sustainable development, and we hope to move forward with these countries as swiftly as possible. But more than just debt relief, we look forward to being there to support their development over the long term.

We believe the best way for the international community to support the poverty reduction strategies of the low-income countries is by opening their markets to the exports of poor countries and by increasing new concessional flows. [Former IMF managing director Horst] Köhler and [World Bank president James] Wolfensohn have indicated that they would gladly join a campaign to convince industrial countries to move to the longstanding UN target for official development assistance of 0.7 percent of GNP within ten years. With current levels of foreign aid at some 0.24 percent of GNP, the difference between the figures is worth $100 billion per year, far more than the net flows generated by even the most ambitious of debt relief proposals. This financing needs to be complemented by greater access to industrial country markets so that developing countries can earn their way in the global economy. These are targets worth pursuing to achieve the International Development Goals.

7

VIEWPOINT

"In developing countries, there . . . are countless horror stories . . . in every arena of privatization."

Forcing Developing Nations to Privatize Public Services in Order to Receive International Loans Harms the Poor

David Moberg

The push by international financial institutions to force poor countries to privatize public services such as water and electrical utilities hurts those who depend on these services, argues David Moberg in the following viewpoint. Nevertheless, to receive international loans, the governments of poor countries have been forced to sell their public services to multinational corporations, some of which raise prices and cut off services to those who cannot pay. Moreover, privatized public services require rigorous government oversight that the newly formed governments of developing nations are often unable to do effectively, Moberg maintains. Moberg is senior editor of *In These Times*, a publication that opposes market-driven policies and supports global justice.

As you read, consider the following questions:

1. According to Moberg, what evidence conflicts with the World Bank's claim that it does not push privatization?
2. What alternatives does economist Tim Kessler argue the World Bank ignores?
3. What impact has the General Agreement on Trade in Services had on public services, in the author's view?

In September 1999, Bolivian officials signed a 40-year contract with a private company named Aguas del Tunari to take over the municipal water system of Cochabamba, the country's third largest city. The company, largely owned by U.S. construction giant Bechtel, was the sole bidder for the contract, which guaranteed 15 percent annual profit in inflation-indexed dollars.

A Celebrated Battleground

With the encouragement of the International Monetary Fund (IMF) and the World Bank, since 1985 Bolivian governments have sold national public assets to foreign investors and opened their markets to global trade. Despite the promise of development by following the "Washington consensus" of economic liberalization, it remained the poorest country in Latin America. But World Bank officials still insisted that Bolivia privatize Cochabamba's water utility and that residents, no matter how poor, pay full cost of the service without subsidy.

Two months after Bechtel's subsidiary took over, it roughly tripled local water rates, telling the poor they could pay one-fourth of their income for water or have the spigot shut off. There were massive protests for several months until the contract was cancelled.

But a few months after signing the contract, Bechtel surreptitiously added new investors and reincorporated its subsidiary in the Netherlands. When it lost the contract, Bechtel sued Bolivia—under terms of a bilateral investment treaty between Bolivia and Netherlands—for damages of at least $25 million for loss of profits it might have made, even though it had invested less than $1 million. Last month [in February 2004], the Bolivian government argued in secret hearings before an investment tribunal affiliated with the World Bank that the treaty doesn't apply, partly because Dutch nationals never controlled Aguas del Tunari.

Cochabamba remains a celebrated battleground in the intensifying worldwide dispute over the privatization of public services, from water and electrical utilities to education, healthcare and pensions. Its ongoing legal struggle reflects the ways in which poor countries often are pressured to privatize a wide range of public assets and services, and then locked into failed policies by international trade agreements.

Free Market Faith

Rich countries—working through international institutions like the World Bank—rarely help poor countries modernize and strengthen public services. But they often push them to privatize and commercialize public services, a move that they themselves would never make. Leading the tide of globalization, international financial institutions are aggressively and undemocratically promoting an ideological agenda of privatization and commercialization.

"The IMF, the World Bank and the World Trade Organization [WTO] care about dismantling the state," says Nancy Alexander, director of the Citizens' Network on Essential Services (CNES), a research and advocacy group. "They're faith-based organizations. They don't care who dismantles the state."

International financial institutions claim that such reforms help reduce poverty, but they often simply are promoting the interests of multinational corporations in water, energy, telecommunications and other industries. Multinational corporate investment in privatization peaked in the late '90s, and many firms have since pulled back in response to protests or financial difficulties. So the World Bank, IMF and related institutions are increasingly offering financial aid, subsidies and guarantees to private multinationals to induce them to privatize.

"In the end, it's not an argument about economics. That's not the bottom line," says Doug Hellinger, executive director of the Development Group on Alternative Policies, which is critical of the IMF and World Bank. "It's ideological, but it's also about giving access to companies on terrific terms. It's really about the IMF representing its northern countries and their corporations."

The World Bank theoretically acknowledges a role for the public sector, but in practice it has pushed privatization since the mid-'80s. This year's budget for water privatization, for example, is triple last year's, and over the past decade the portion of the bank's lending for water projects tied to privatization soared. In 2002 it adopted a strategy that emphasized development led by private corporations, and it works closely with the WTO to impose on poor countries the kinds of pro-corporate policies richer countries have the freedom to negotiate.

Exerting Indirect Pressure

When countries suffer from financial crises or crippling debt, the IMF and World Bank often insist on privatization of state-owned enterprises, utilities and social services as a condition for financial help. But sometimes, Alexander explains, they push privatization indirectly. For example, they typically require cuts in government budgets, public services and aid to localities. They press for decentralization of public services, dismantling of utilities into smaller units, assessment of market prices for services and elimination of cross-subsidies that may reduce costs for the poor. Financially squeezed by these policies, municipalities may be tempted to privatize the decentralized services. The multinationals then cherry pick the most profitable pieces serving more affluent urban areas, leaving the government responsible for poor and unprofitable rural areas or urban shantytowns.

While some public services in developing countries work well, others are deeply flawed. But as CNES economist Tim Kessler argues, the World Bank acts as if the only alternative is privatization, not improving public services with outside financial and technical aid and with greater citizen accountability. In any case, privatized utilities need strong public regulation, which is difficult and expensive to do well. Paradoxically, weak and corrupt governments, whose public services could most benefit from reform, are least able to regulate privatized systems. Often they sell public goods on the cheap to cronies and patrons, making privatization really "briberization," says former World Bank chief economist Joseph Stiglitz.

Management Matters

Advocates argue that privatization increases efficiency and investment, fosters competition, shrinks deficits and improves services. There are many instances, such as in Chile, where privatized public enterprises increased efficiency and improved service. But in developed countries public utilities generally are as efficient as or better than private.

Water as a Human Right vs. Water as an Economic Good

Human beings can survive one month without food but not one week without water. For this reason, human societies in all parts of the world have valued water as life itself and have recognized in various international covenants and declarations the right to water as a fundamental human right. . . .

Of late, this basic right to water has come under threat not only from increasing environmental degradation and the consequent backlash on water resources but because a handful of transnational corporations, creditor banks, governments of industrialized countries, international financial institutions, etc. are pushing privatization as a solution to this crisis. This has resulted in a shift of functions and responsibilities in water provisioning from the state to the private sector where the water industry is no longer a basic element of human life to which everyone has a right to but as another economic good that can be sold for a profit to those with the means to pay its price. Supplying water to people and companies worldwide has in fact grown to a $400-billion industry on a global scale.

Mae Buenaventura, Bubut Palattao, and Lidy Nacpil, *Jubilee South*, December 12, 2003.

In developing countries, there also are countless horror stories of price gouging, poor service, meager investment and discrimination against the poor from every continent and in every arena of privatization. For example, Suez, one of two multinationals controlling at least 70 percent of the world's private water contracts, recently lost or abandoned water operations in Argentina, Phillipines and Puerto Rico once hailed as model successes. A newly released study by a network of citizens groups that collaborated with the World Bank, "Structural Adjustment: The SAPRI [Structural Adjustment Participatory Review Initiative] Report," concluded that privatization did not accelerate growth and the form of ownership did not determine efficiency of services as much as management policy.

Despite the failures of privatization, the World Bank and IMF have not shifted their focus to strengthening and democratizing public services. Instead, they are increasing funding to subsidize, to commercially guarantee and to promote privatization (as head of an expert panel on water infrastructure sponsored by the World Bank and multinational water companies). Former IMF managing director Michel Camdessus . . . recommended . . . that there should be more subsidies and guarantees for water privatizers and that the bank should deal more with state and local governments (which typically are less savvy in negotiating with giant multinationals than national governments).

At the WTO, the richer countries want to include more services under the General Agreement on Trade in Services (GATS), potentially opening historically public functions to competition that would benefit multinational service corporations and would indirectly privatize. Once a service is opened under GATS, countries cannot reverse course—for example, make healthcare an exclusively public service—without paying every country that claims it lost a trade opportunity. GATS rules also would severely restrict domestic regulation of service industries.

If the rich countries, along with the World Bank, IMF and WTO, persist in their current privatizing strategies, Cochabamba may turn out to have been an early skirmish in a much wider war.

VIEWPOINT

"The patent system is a raw deal for developing countries—because it gives them monopoly prices without giving them innovation."

International Patent Laws Hurt Developing Nations

Amy Kapczynski

Strict international patent laws make many drugs too expensive for people in developing nations to purchase, argues Amy Kapczynski in the following viewpoint. Using patent laws as justification, pharmaceutical companies in rich nations are trying to prevent poor nations from developing cheaper versions of drugs needed to fight epidemics such as AIDS, she maintains. Kapczynski contends that the debate over international patent laws highlights the most serious problem with globalization: It permits affluent nations to set the terms of global agreements to the detriment of poor nations. Kapczynski was an AIDS activist while a law student at Yale University.

As you read, consider the following questions:

1. According to Kapczynski, what are the two dirty secrets about patents?
2. In the author's opinion, how did the U.S. Congress threaten to use compulsory licensing when faced with a potential public health crisis?
3. Why is globalization not an equalizing phenomenon, in the author's view?

Amy Kapczynski, "Strict International Patent Laws Hurt Developing Countries," *YaleGlobal*, December 16, 2002.

[In 2001] at a conference about health and human rights, a representative from a pharmaceutical company told the audience a joke. It was about the now infamous lawsuit that 39 pharmaceutical companies brought against the South African government. The lawsuit was intended to stop the government from making cheaper medicines available in their country—and in the context of the HIV/AIDS pandemic, it generated global outrage. After three years of obstructing the implementation of the South African law, the companies were forced to abandon the lawsuit, which had become a PR nightmare. Here's the joke: "People ask me," the representative said, "how we could have been so stupid as to sue Nelson Mandela. I tell them: We had to. Mother Theresa was already dead."

Perhaps not a terribly funny joke, but it usefully highlights a seismic shift in global public awareness and opinion that happened recently. In 1998, when the 39 companies filed their suit, it seemed to them a perfectly good idea to sue Nelson Mandela to stop him from encroaching upon their patents. Even [former vice president] Al Gore supported the lawsuit, traveling to South Africa to threaten the government with trade sanctions if they did not revoke the law. Three years later, that same lawsuit came to be seen akin to an assault upon a saint. How did this happen, and what have we learned from it? What was the South African lawsuit about, and what does it tell us about globalization?

The Patent System

Understanding the lawsuit requires a bit of background. Patents are temporary monopolies granted by governments. They give the inventor a right to exclude everyone else from producing, selling, or distributing a product in that country. Monopolies are generally viewed as a bad thing, because they create what economists call "deadweight losses." So why are governments granting them? The theory is that the higher prices that patents allow companies to charge provide incentives to develop and commercialize new products. The dirty secret about patents, as a law school professor of mine once put it, is that no one knows how strong patents have to be to serve this purpose. For example, are twenty years of patent protection necessary to provide sufficient incentives for research? Or is ten years sufficient? Under international rules, patents must now be granted for a minimum of twenty years—although until recently, patents were often much shorter, even in the U.S.

Here is another dirty secret: Patents cannot generate innovation where there is no market. Even with patents, it is not profitable for companies to produce drugs for diseases that primarily affect the poor. So, for example, only 13 out of the 1393 new drugs approved between 1975 and 1999 were for tropical diseases, which is to say, diseases that primarily affect poorer regions of the world. This suggests that the patent system is a raw deal for developing countries—because it gives them monopoly prices without giving them innovation. It also suggests a need for substantial public funds for drug development for neglected diseases.

The AIDS Crisis

Cut to South Africa in 1998: Approximately one in five adults is living with HIV/AIDS. Since 1996, the world has known that "cocktails" of antiretroviral drugs save lives. They are not a cure for AIDS, but here they have turned it into an almost chronic disease, akin to diabetes. The rate of AIDS deaths in the U.S. was plummeting, but in South Africa, no one except the exceedingly rich could afford the drugs. In the U.S., taxpayers subsidize the cost of the drugs, which cost around $15,000 per year. In South Africa, making treatment universally available at such prices would have bankrupted the government. But it was not the drugs themselves that were expensive—it was the patents. Where there are no patents on these drugs, as is the case in India, for example, you can buy equivalent versions of those $15,000 drugs for $200. India does not currently grant patents for products (pharmaceutical or otherwise), although they soon will have to, according to an agreement which all WTO [World Trade Organization] members must sign and adhere to, known as the "TRIPS"—Trade-Related Aspects of Intellectual Property—Agreement.

The South African government was in a bind. South Africa has a strong patent system—the legacy of apartheid, but also the result of pressure from countries like the United States. Affordable drugs existed, but not for them. So, in 1998, they did what any responsible government would do: They passed a law that would give them the power to bring drug prices down. The law would have allowed them to "parallel import" cheaper medicines—that is, to take advantage of the fact that patented drugs are sold at different prices in different countries. Parallel importing is what busloads of senior US citizens do when they go to Canada to fill their prescriptions—buying the same brand-name drugs in a country where they are less expensive. And it's completely legal under the TRIPS agreement.

The Compulsory Licensing Strategy

The South African law might also have given the government the power to use generic drugs, harnessing the power of competition to drive prices down. The TRIPS Agreement allows governments to override patents and allow generic production, through a strategy known as "compulsory licensing." Governments can use compulsory licensing whenever they choose, as long as they follow certain procedures (which include first negotiating with the patent-holder and allowing appeal of the government's decision). In an emergency, or where the product is for public non-commercial use, a government can issue a compulsory license without even consulting the patent-holder.

A Bolshevik notion? Piracy? Only if you consider the U.S. Congress to be communists and pirates. During the anthrax crisis last year [2001], Congress threatened to use compulsory licensing to obtain the antibiotic Cipro more cheaply and quickly from generic manufacturers. Bayer, who holds the patent on Cipro, immediately offered to dramatically lower its prices and increase production.

Faced with a potential public health crisis, Congress recognized what many other countries have been arguing all along: that patents are not "rights" but rather privileges—and that they do not come before the rights to health and life. But that is not how they—or the drug industry—approached the issue when it came to South Africa. The possibility that South Africa—a tiny percentage of the world's drug market—might start using generic drugs was treated as a colossal threat to the interests of the U.S. pharmaceutical industry. It did not matter that the United States had signed the TRIPS agreement in 1994, recognizing that developing country governments have the ability to do just what the U.S. would later do with Cipro. And it didn't matter that literally millions of lives were at stake. According to Charlene Barshefsky, the U.S. Trade Representative at the time: "We all missed it. . . . I didn't appreciate at all the extent to which our interpretation of South Africa's international property obligations were draconian."

Countering the Claims of Pharmaceutical Companies

Anti-retroviral medicines are an effective means of treating HIV/AIDS, but high prices due to patents make it impossible for people of the developing world to gain access to these life-saving medicines. Pharmaceutical companies argue that high prices are critical to fund research and development. However, studies demonstrate that funding for 5 out of the 6 anti-retroviral drugs is mainly provided by national governments. In addition, companies also claim that the length of time needed to approve new drugs is another significant reason for high prices. However, anti-retrovirals are usually approved within 44.6 months, the shortest time for approval of any class of drugs.

Furthermore, research and development investment for the health needs of people in the developing world has nearly disappeared. Developing countries, which represent 75% of the world population, account for less than 10% of the global pharmaceutical market. Pharmaceutical companies invest more resources to develop medicines to treat what some call lifestyle diseases such as obesity, baldness, and impotence. These companies are hardly interested in developing drugs that address diseases like malaria or tuberculosis which plague 75% of the world population.

Ifeoma Opara, *TransAfrica Forum Globalization Monitor*, Spring 2004.

Activists around the world realized it, and mobilized against the lawsuit with slogans like "Patient Rights Over Patent Rights," and "Stop Medical Apartheid." In March, 2001, when the case finally reached the courtroom, the drug companies, fearing the public relations backlash, withdrew their suit.

Riding on the momentum of this win, and with the example of Cipro now in hand, developing countries successfully secured affirmation at the WTO Ministerial meeting in Doha in November, 2001, that they have the right to parallel import and issue compulsory licenses, and that the TRIPS Agreement should be "interpreted and implemented in a manner supportive of WTO Members' right to protect public health and, in particular, to promote access to medicines for all."

Imposing Draconian Laws

End of story? Not exactly. The lesson that the Clinton Administration learned has been lost on the Bush Administration. They are reneging on promises made at Doha, trying to impose draconian intellectual property laws onto countries through multilateral agreements such as the Free Trade of the Americas Act and bilateral agreements like those recently negotiated with Chile and Singapore. The USTR [United States Trade Representative] has just announced plans for a regional African agreement known as the Southern African Free Trade and Development Agreement, or SAFTDA (with South Africa, Botswana, Lesotho, Namibia, and Swaziland), and seeks a similar agreement with ASEAN [Association of Southeast Asian Nation] countries. If the U.S. negotiating position remains consistent—as it has done up until this point—the USTR will seek TRIPS-plus provisions (that is, more protective of patent rights and more restrictive of countries' abilities to use generic drugs) in each of these agreements, with devastating long-term consequences for the health of people, and especially poor people, in these countries.

The Bush Administration has also prevented a positive resolution to one crucial issue left unresolved at Doha. Currently, TRIPS allows countries to produce generic drugs through compulsory licensing, but requires that such drugs be used predominantly for the country's domestic market. That means that countries cannot export generic products thus produced—even to countries where there are no patents, and these generics are perfectly legal. This undermines the logic of free trade that the WTO is based upon. That logic, which often goes by the heading of "comparative advantage," contends that countries will benefit in the aggregate if each specializes and trades in what they are best at. Thus, you would expect to find WTO proponents insisting that countries like Brazil and India, which have strong generic markets, should be able to supply the markets of other countries if they can do it most cheaply. Many of the poorest countries have no indigenous capacity to manufacture pharmaceuticals, and thus they will need to import if they are to make use of generic drugs. At Doha, governments noted this issue and promised to find a resolution to the issue. . . . That deadline has passed, but no agreement has yet been reached because the governments of the U.S. and other wealthy countries have insisted on unheard-of limitations and WTO oversight of any exports; for example, that such exports be limited to certain diseases and be pre-approved by the WTO.

What does all this tell us about globalization? That it is still far too easy for powerful countries like the United States to set the terms of global agreements and to ignore those terms when they find them inconvenient. The same applies to the large multi-national companies who search for mega-profits to the exclusion of all other considerations. Another lesson is that globalization isn't an equalizing phenomenon. As shown here, U.S. rules, interests, and ignorance can be writ large upon other areas of the world. Nonetheless, it is also clear that if activists mobilize across borders to resist inequitable outcomes, they can change the rules of globalization—not for good, but for the better.

Periodical Bibliography

The following articles have been selected to supplement the diverse views presented in this chapter.

Michael Albert — "What Are We For?" *ZNet*, September 6, 2001. www.zmag.org.

Gary S. Becker — "How Globalization Helps the Poor," *Business Week*, April 21, 2003.

Jagdish N. Bhagwati — "What Enriches the Poor and Liberates the Oppressed?" *Times* (London), March 5, 2004.

Paul Blustein — "Free Trade's Muddy Waters," *Washington Post*, July 13, 2003.

Alison Brysk — "Globalization and Human Rights: It's a Small World After All," *Phi Kappa Phi Forum*, Fall 2003.

Ron Chepesiuk — "Ready-Made Misery," *Toward Freedom*, Spring 2004.

Larry Elliott — "The Lost Decade: They Were Promised a Brighter Future, but in the 1990s, the World's Poor Fell Further Behind," *Guardian*, July 9, 2003.

Aaron Goldzimer — "Worse than the World Bank? Export Credit Agencies—the Secret Engine of Globalization," *Food First Backgrounder*, Winter 2003.

Nat Hentoff — "Financing Mass Murder: How Free-Market Investors Contribute to Genocide in Darfur While They Take the Profits," *Village Voice*, October 8, 2004.

International Monetary Fund — "Globalization: Threat or Opportunity?" April 12, 2000. www.imf.org.

David Malpass — "We Grow, They Grow," *Wall Street Journal*, November 3, 2004.

Enver Masud — "Corporate Globalization Threatens World's Poor, Middle Class," *Wisdom Fund*, October 10, 2000. www.twf.org.

Mahathir bin Mohamad — "Globalization and Developing Countries," *Globalist*, October 10, 2002.

Alvin Powell — "Does Foreign Aid Aid? Discuss," *Harvard University Gazette*, October 18, 2001.

Judy Rebick — "Anti-Globalization/Anti-Fundamentalism," *ZNet*, March 12, 2002. www.zmag.org.

Ruth Rosenbaum "Under the Heel of Business," *Sojourners*, January 2000.

Tina Rosenberg "So Far, Globalization Has Failed the World's Poor. But It's Not Trade That Has Hurt Them. It's a Rigged System. The Free-Trade Fix," *New York Times Magazine*, August 18, 2002.

Peter D. Sutherland "Why We Should Embrace Globalization," *Finance & Development*, September 2002.

Robert Weissman "Grotesque Inequality: Corporate Globalization and the Global Gap Between Rich and Poor," *Multinational Monitor*, July/August 2003.

CHAPTER 4

What Global Policies Are Best?

Chapter Preface

One of several controversies in the debate over which global policies are best is how to regulate the activities of multinational corporations (MNCs). In their quest to compete in the global marketplace and produce the most competitively priced products, some MNCs have production facilities in developing countries such as China where labor is cheap and regulation of workplace conditions is limited or nonexistent. In 2000 the National Labor Committee, a nonprofit organization dedicated to promoting and defending human and worker rights in the global economy, reported that workers in China producing handbags for Wal-Mart were beaten by guards for being late; those producing Huffy bicycles worked fifteen-hour shifts, seven days a week without overtime, and sixteen-year-old girls making shoes for Stride Rite applied toxic glues with their bare hands.

Public awareness about sweatshop conditions in overseas factories grew during the late 1990s. One of the first and most visible MNCs targeted by activists was Nike Corporation. Workers who made 1.2 million pairs of Nike sneakers each month were paid $2.23 a day while working in an abysmal Indonesian factory. The publicity from this case set into motion a global movement against such production facilities and a demand for corporate accountability. According to global governance analyst Ann Florini, "The lack of effective international (and often national) regulation to protect workers, communities, and the environment has spurred the development of a powerful movement aimed at promoting corporate social responsibility." In response, some MNCs have taken the initiative to establish corporate codes of conduct. However, critics claim these efforts are inadequate to protect the human rights of workers.

Faced with public outrage and consumer pressure, many MNCs have created socially responsible corporate codes of conduct. Those who support such codes, Florini maintains, "see them as a valuable way to get corporations to buy into new norms of behavior without the need for government intervention, making them attractive to corporate leaders who want to fend off government regulation." The codes both protect company reputations and reassure consumers that the company's production processes ensure decent working conditions.

Opponents contend that such codes are flawed. They claim that the standards are voluntary, and that there is no mechanism for enforcement. According to EarthRights International, "No government will monitor these corporations' compliance, and a failure to comply will subject them to the court of public opinion, and no other court. And that's assuming the public learns of any infractions." Even those codes that call for external monitoring are controversial. Once such codes have been established, "an independent external auditor comes in, assesses whether a company is in full compliance, and if so certifies it," Florini explains. Compliance, however, is voluntary. "No government enforces them; no international organization has made the standards law. Instead," Florini, maintains, "the assumption is that corporations will want to be so certified because they will find it good for business—because consumers will prefer to buy certified products."

Moreover, critics question the ethics of the external auditors themselves. Environment and labor policy professor Dara O'Rourke challenged the effectiveness of one of the leading social accounting firms, PricewaterhouseCoopers, in his report, *Monitoring the Monitors: A Critique of PricewaterhouseCoopers (PwC's) Labor Monitoring*. "PwC's monitoring efforts are significantly flawed," O'Rourke maintains. His report found that when one auditor found some of the questions "embarrassing," she skipped them. The auditor also answered some questions herself without asking workers. In one factory the factory president selected the workers to be interviewed. Claims O'Rourke, "PwC's audit reports glossed over problems of freedom of association and collective bargaining, overlooked serious violations of health and safety standards, and failed to report common problems in wages and hours."

Multinational corporations are increasingly being held to higher standards in the global marketplace. However, "the dispute over exactly what those standards should be—and who should decide—has just begun," concludes Florini. Whether corporate codes of conduct are adequate to protect workers' rights remains controversial. The authors in the following chapter debate the effectiveness of other controversial global policies.

Viewpoint 1

"Instead of being opposed to globalization, progressives [in America] should pressure the world's wealthiest nations into sharing the benefits."

The United States Should Promote Globalization

Robert Reich

The United States should abandon isolationist policies and support initiatives that promote globalization, argues Robert Reich in the following viewpoint. The Bush administration, Reich claims, has retreated from global cooperation and trade. Reich contends that America must remove trade and investment barriers and strengthen international institutions that were created to spread global wealth and promote public and environmental health, especially in poor nations. Reich, a professor of social and economic policy, served as secretary of labor under President Bill Clinton and is author of *The Work of Nations*.

As you read, consider the following questions:

1. According to Reich, what has been the impact of protesters' failure to communicate what aspects of globalization they are against?
2. What shaped U.S. foreign policy after World War II, in the author's opinion?
3. In the author's view, what has grown alongside the global economy?

Robert Reich, "A Proper Global Agenda," *The American Prospect*, vol. 12, September 24, 2001, p. 48.

These days, any official organization with the word "International," "World," or "Global" in its title has to worry about where it meets, check in with the riot police, and pray for rain. . . .

Global protesters haven't communicated clearly to the rest of the world exactly what they're against. As a result, the protests are seen by many as part of a growing revulsion toward globalization in general.

Antiglobal Forces

[President] George W. Bush, meanwhile, is mounting his own protest against globalization—trashing the Kyoto treaty on climate change,[1] junking the Anti-Ballistic Missile Treaty, indefinitely deferring Senate ratification of the 1996 nuclear test-ban treaty and the 1993 nuclear weapons-reduction treaty, diluting a United Nations agreement to reduce illegal trafficking of small arms, and taking a decidedly low profile in Israel and other settings of ethnic violence.

Since the United States is the biggest and strongest country, Bush figures, why should we be constrained in any way? He tells Russian President Vladimir Putin that he's happy to negotiate an end to the ABM treaty as long as the Russians agree with us. The State Department dubs this sort of America-first unilateralism "a la carte multilateralism"—we choose, and other nations agree.

Superficially, there's an eerie overlapping of the antiglobal forces inside and outside the White House. Some of the troops on the street appear to share Bush's disdain for international entanglements and institutions of whatever kind. So does the Republican Party's small-town Main Street wing—which doesn't trust Wall Street, doesn't particularly like global corporations, and doesn't want to mix with too many foreigners.

The Development of Globalization

After World War II, U.S. foreign policy was shaped by a coalition of big corporations and fierce anticommunists that

1. The Kyoto Protocol is an agreement made by industrialized nations to reduce emissions believed to lead to global warming.

wanted America to play an assertive role in the world. These folks were behind the creation of the World Bank, International Monetary Fund, United Nations, General Agreement on Tariffs and Trade, and North Atlantic Treaty Organization.[2] They fought global communism, made the world safe for U.S. companies, propped up right-wing dictatorships, and enhanced living standards in many parts of the world. Even the AFL-CIO [a powerful American labor union] of that era spent more energy berating communism and encouraging free-trade unions abroad than it did organizing here at home.

But global communism is no longer a threat, and the large corporations that spread American capitalism have morphed into global behemoths that have no special affiliation with the United States other than their mailing address. One of America's "big three" automakers is German, and the fourth-largest is Japanese. Global capital sloshes wherever the return is highest. In economic terms, it's harder than ever to tell who "us" is.

So no one should be surprised that the Republican isolationists are back on the ascent and the White House is preaching America-first unilateralism. But the left mustn't side with them—or even appear to do so. Instead of being opposed to globalization, progressives should pressure the world's wealthiest nations into sharing the benefits. While the global economy has grown at an average rate of 2.3 percent a year during the past three decades, the gap between the best-off and worst-off countries (as measured in per capita gross national product) is 10 times wider now than it was 30 years ago. And with poverty comes disease—AIDS already has claimed the lives of 10 million Africans and is projected to kill 25 million more over the next decade—as well as the continued destruction of the global environment.

Encouraging Globalization

Rather than advocate for less trade, progressives should seek to remove barriers that make it difficult for poorer countries

2. Created after World War II, the organizations and treaties listed are global institutions designed to foster economic cooperation.

to export to richer ones. That means fewer subsidies to farmers in advanced nations, combined with lower tariffs on farm products from the third world and fewer barriers (including "voluntary restraint agreements") to textile and steel imports from poor nations.

Promoting the Voices of Globalization

We must be clear and specific about what globalization means in our view. We need to calm the rhetoric if we expect our loyal opposition to do the same.

One way to do that is amplify the chorus of those individual voices worldwide. Those individuals . . . that are in the middle of globalization.

Like the Costa Rican farmer who gets an internet connection, finds out what his crop's really worth, and sells to the best bidder.

Or the Congo artisan who bypasses the profit pyramid and sells direct to the world on websites like Viatru.

Or the Missouri entrepreneur whose oak barrels used to store only bourbon in Kentucky but now hold Scotch in Scotland and wine in South Africa and France.

Or the 70 percent of our small business customers who tell us that they've seen an increase in sales due to their web presence. These same customers tell us that nearly 40 percent of their online sales come from brand new customers.

Ladies and gentlemen, we need to promote these voices.

These are the voices that will give globalization the traction it needs to move forward.

Michael Eskew, *Vital Speeches of the Day*, June 1, 2002.

Instead of seeking less global investment, we should demand that more of it—especially in manufacturing plants and equipment—be directed toward countries that need help. And by international agreement, capital flight should be prevented or slowed by means of a small transaction tax.

Rather than try to weaken international institutions, we should push them in a different direction. We need a World Bank that coordinates real debt relief for third-world nations; an IMF [International Monetary Fund] that conditions loans on investments in education and strong social safety nets rather than on fiscal austerity; a global patent office that forces drug manufacturers to slash prices on pharmaceuticals needed by poor nations; a global health institution capable of attacking AIDS and cracking down on the trafficking of women and children for prostitution; a world environmental agency that imposes strict emissions rules; and an international peacekeeping force that responds immediately to tribal genocide.

This is no time to retreat from globalization. The left should visibly and vocally engage in the world on behalf of a more vigorous and humane system of international governance.

"It is going to be up to informed U.S. citizens to reverse the dangerous international drive toward global socialism."

The United States Should Not Promote Globalization

Jennifer A. Gritt

Americans must prevent efforts by international unions and trade organizations to equalize the world's economies at the expense of America's economic strength, maintains Jennifer A. Gritt in the following viewpoint. Economic policies designed to further integrate the United States into the global economy are harming American businesses, she asserts. According to Gritt, the United States must set economic policies that benefit America, not other nations. Gritt is a freelance writer from Appleton, Wisconsin.

As you read, consider the following questions:

1. What evidence does Gritt cite to prove that the Bush administration is trying to socialize America's economy?
2. According to the author, why do international organizations need to further degrade America's manufacturing base?
3. In the author's opinion, how can the power of the European Union be limited?

Jennifer A. Gritt, "EU Rising," *New American*, vol. 20, January 12, 2004, p. 27.

In November [2003], the World Trade Organization (WTO) ruled that the 30 percent tariff President [George W.] Bush imposed on imported steel in March 2002 violated international trade rules and was therefore illegal. The WTO, however, had no way of enforcing its ruling by itself. So the European Union (EU), acting on behalf of the WTO, rose up to enforce that organization's ruling against the U.S. for the supposed purpose of leveling the economic playing field for Europe.

Soon after the WTO ruling, the EU began mobilizing against the U.S., threatening to implement $2.2 billion worth of retaliatory tariffs if the Bush administration failed to abide by the trade body's wishes. It worked. On December 3, [2003] President Bush announced that he would repeal the steel tariff. "It's a great sign for the EU that it can make the US sit up and take notice," Digby Jones, director-general of the Confederation of British Industry, told the December 2 *London Guardian.* "America can be a force for good in trade and the world economy but not when it is indulging in a bout of protectionism."

Protecting Global Trade

But the issue here is not free trade vs. protectionism. Rather, it's the ongoing effort by internationalists in the WTO, the EU—and even our own federal government—to destroy America's ability to determine its own trade policies. . . .

Tariff or no tariff, the disintegration of the American manufacturing sector was set in motion the moment international socialism took root in Washington and the U.S. became party to international organizations such as the UN [United Nations] and the WTO. Artfully misnamed free-trade agreements, such as NAFTA [North American Free Trade Agreement] and the proposed FFAA [Free Trade Area of the Americas], are designed to accelerate the process.

According to a . . . study by the National Association of Manufacturers (NAM), "the position of U.S. manufacturers in global trade has shown a marked deterioration in the last five years." America, the report continues, now has a "trade deficit in the goods sector equal to one-quarter of all output of the domestic manufacturing sector. At the same time, the

U.S. share of global export markets has fallen from a high of nearly 14 percent in the 1990s to about 10.7 percent in 2002." NAM also points out that the fact that "the U.S. manufacturing sector . . . now finds itself mired in a slow recovery leads to the inescapable conclusion that cost pressures outside manufacturers' direct control have conspired to threaten the U.S. manufacturing leadership."

Weakening America's Economic Strength

Yet the neoconservative Bush administration is doing nothing to try and offset or reverse this trend. Why? Because President Bush and his internationalist administration don't want to slow down the process of U.S. integration into the global economy—integration that can only happen if America's economic strength is weakened and brought to the level of European industries. In other words, America's economy must be socialized on a global scale.

A case in point would be the Bush administration's vow—in lieu of keeping the steel tariff—to continue to monitor steel imports in order to detect any flooding of imported steel into American markets. According to a December 3, [2003] ABC news report, Alan Wolff, a Washington-based attorney representing U.S. steel companies, stated: "The White House knows the U.S. industry still confronts serious issues including massive global overcapacity and a whole variety of foreign subsidies that encourage this over-capacity." The report went on to state that "steel officials said the [Bush] administration likely would pledge to continue international talks for reducing excess global steel capacity and reining in subsidies that foreign governments provide for their domestic steel companies."

While this sounds like President Bush is making an effort to protect the steel industry, in reality the administration is doing little more than paying lip service to American interests as it works to build a WTO-headed system of global managed trade.

They Have Only Just Begun

In addition to the WTO ruling on Bush's steel tariff, other economic decisions made by the Bush administration are coming under international scrutiny as well. For example, the American practice of offering a tax break for American companies if they set up subsidiaries abroad was put on the WTO's docket. As reported by CNSNEWS.com on December 5, [2003] "The WTO also ruled against the U.S. in that case last month, and Europe has planned retaliation worth hundreds of millions of dollars starting next March." Steven Everts of the London-based Center for European Reform, drawing a comparison to the tariff ruling, stressed: "There's certainly a similar pattern. At some point in time, the U.S. will have to amend its legislation to resolve the issue."

Another area where the U.S. might run into trouble with the EU is the . . . decision to bar countries which did not support the Bush administration's invasion of Iraq from being allowed to submit contract bids for reconstruction efforts. According to a December 12 *Reuters* report, EU leaders appear to be split on whether the international body should retaliate, not committing either way to whether or not they would move forward with counter measures.

Equalizing American and European Economies

Why—with all the U.S. efforts to homogenize the global economy over the past several years—would the WTO and EU need to further degrade America's manufacturing base? Because the socialized economies of Europe are still unable to match the manufacturing might of the U.S., which—despite decades of socialist impositions by Washington—remains vigorous because of its free market foundations.

According to a December 10 *PRNewswire* report, the European Commission recently released a study documenting the widespread productivity slowdown throughout Europe's industrial sectors. The study's findings "suggest that strong productivity growth—a powerful sign of economic growth, health and efficiency—is underway in the U.S. not only among information and communication technology (ICT) manufacturers, but also for major users of this technology, especially services. In the EU, only producers or intensive users of ICT have experienced an improvement in productivity growth, and the acceleration is far less than achieved in the US."

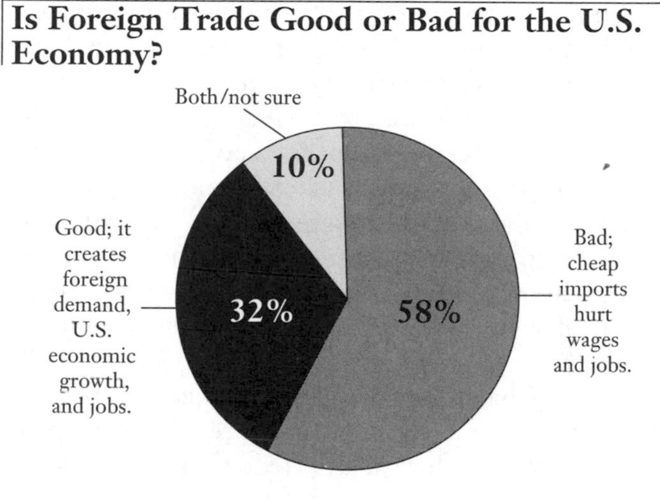

Wall Street Journal/NBC News poll conducted by Peter Hart and Robert Teeter, *Wall Street Journal*, December 10, 1998.

So in order for the EU to equalize the American and European economies, the U.S. manufacturing base must be further eroded in order to give European and other foreign nations the chance to catch up. In addition to taking measures to stunt economic growth in America, the EU recently approved an $80 billion investment plan for public works projects throughout Europe that is reminiscent of Franklin D. Roosevelt's socialist New Deal. In a joint statement made by 25 current and soon-to-be EU members, the economic package "is an important step . . . to improve competitiveness, employment and the enlarged union's growth potential."

Do Not Be Fooled

For some, the breakdown of the . . . EU summit in Brussels and the failure to adopt a formal constitution were signs that the power of the European body is in decline. But a closer look into the supposed summit failure reveals that the EU is only haggling over just how centralized its power should initially be. In May 2004, EU membership will increase from 15 to 25, with the majority of the former Soviet satellite states in Eastern Europe joining the European government. The major point of contention at the . . . summit was the unwillingness of

Spain and Poland to give up their generous voting rights. According to a December 13 EU press release: "The draft text proposes a new 'double majority' system, under which decisions would require backing from a majority of member states representing 60 percent of the EU's population—a formula that boosts the EU heavyweights' voting power."

While Spain and Poland were unwilling to compromise on the proposed voting system, both Germany and France were not deterred in the drive toward unifying Europe under a single constitution. According to a December 14 Associated Press account, "[French president Jacques] Chirac and German Chancellor Gerhard Schroeder spoke of the need for a core group of countries to press ahead with closer integration," which they acknowledged has a tendency to raise "fears over the cohesion of the EU."

And not every dispute ended in failure. As reported by the December 14 *New York Times*, "The meeting was not without successes. On Friday, the leaders took a first important step toward striking a deal on the constitution's draft text . . . when they agreed unanimously to a common defense policy that included planning abilities independent of NATO [North Atlantic Treaty Organization]," a measure that would diminish American influence over European defense. "Europe is not in crisis," Chirac insisted in response to the failed summit. "Europe has institutions, Europe will expand. Europe works."

Despite its intramural squabbles, the EU appears to be fast becoming a global force capable of enforcing WTO resolutions and dictating the economic policies of the U.S. But it should be remembered that the EU—like the WTO and the UN—only has the power Washington is willing to surrender to it. And in the most recent trade dispute, President Bush took a dive in order to set an important precedent on the road to creating a socialist global trade system.

It is going to be up to informed U.S. citizens to reverse the dangerous international drive toward global socialism by restoring the power of Congress to rein in the out-of-control Executive Branch that has been predominantly responsible for building the internationalist foundation for America's political and economic destruction.

VIEWPOINT 3

"We must begin to make a U-turn: away from globalization and toward the strengthening of local and national economies."

Local Economies Should Be Protected from Globalization

Helena Norberg-Hodge

Globalization harms developing countries and leads to global environmental degradation, claims Helena Norberg-Hodge in the following viewpoint. As nations globalize, she argues, farmers move to cities to produce goods for the global marketplace. Living in cities, the poor can no longer meet their families' needs by raising their own food, Norberg-Hodge asserts. Moreover, shipping goods across the globe leads to increased consumption of fossil fuels and the destructive global warming that accompanies it. Norberg-Hodge is director of the International Society of Ecology and Culture, which promotes local alternatives to global consumer culture.

As you read, consider the following questions:

1. According to Norberg-Hodge, how is localization accomplished?
2. In the author's opinion, what is required to prevent further urbanization in the Southern Hemisphere?
3. What are the potential consequences of allowing globalization to continue uncontrolled, in the author's view?

Helena Norberg-Hodge, "The Case for Localization," *Earth Island Journal*, vol. 17, Spring 2002, p. 47.

Across the world, deregulation is leading to a breakdown of local enterprise and ever-greater dependence on long-distance trade and transport. This in turn means ever-increasing consumption of fossil fuels. So globalization is directly and inextricably linked to climate change.

Strengthening Rural Life

If we want to avoid the havoc and hardship that further climate change will inevitably bring, we must begin to make a U-turn: away from globalization and toward the strengthening of local and national economies. Since globalization goes hand-in-hand with urbanization, this means actively working to protect and strengthen rural life.

Localization is about shortening the distance between producers and consumers. It is not about eliminating all trade, but rather about reducing to an absolute minimum the exorbitant waste now caused by having everything from butter to raw logs crisscrossing the globe.

Localization needs to happen simultaneously in both the North and the South.[1] As things stand today, roughly 50 percent of the world's population is still rurally based—the majority of them are in the South. It is vital that everything is done to prevent this proportion from declining.

A common assumption, even among environmentalists, is that the nations of the South need a little more time to catch up with the North (in other words, more access to global markets) before they can be expected to reduce their fossil fuel consumption and begin to localize. But such thinking flies in the face of reality. Contrary to the propaganda, the global economy cannot possibly enable villagers in rural China or Bangladesh to live the life of middle-class Westerners. For the vast majority, it cannot even provide the most basic needs of housing, education, clothing, health care, nutrition and employment. As recent experience has shown, what globalization does do is increase the gap between rich and poor, pulling vast numbers of people away

1. In this context, North means nations in the Northern Hemisphere, most of which are economically developed. South means nations in the Southern Hemisphere, most of which are poor.

from the land into squalid urban slums.

If, like the North, the South had colonies to exploit, the situation might be different. But they don't—and simple arithmetic tells us that it's impossible for everyone to emulate a model that allows people to use vastly more than their fair share of the Earth's resources.

A History of Protecting Local Interests

Just after the colonies won their freedom, the mother country suggested that the United States trade what we produced best and, in exchange, Britain would trade back with what it produced best. . . . Alexander Hamilton, in his famous "Report on Manufactures,". . . said, we are not going to remain your colony shipping you our natural resources—rice, cotton, indigo, timber, iron ore—and importing your manufactured products. We are going to build our own manufacturing capacity.

The second bill ever adopted by Congress, on July 4, 1789, was a 50 percent tariff on numerous articles. This policy of protectionism, endorsed by James Madison and Thomas Jefferson, continued under President [Abraham] Lincoln when he launched America's steel industry by refusing to import from England the steel for the Transcontinental Railroad. President Franklin Roosevelt protected agriculture, President [Dwight] Eisenhower protected oil and President [John F.] Kennedy protected textiles. This economic and industrial giant, the United States, was built on protectionism and, for more than a century, financed it with tariffs. And it worked.

Ernest F. Hollings, *Washington Post*, March 21, 2004.

In the rural villages of the South, life can be undeniably hard. But villagers can at least grow a few vegetables, maybe keep some chickens or even a cow, and they can rely on friends and family for help with agricultural work. In the slums of the big cities, by contrast, they suddenly become dependent on hard cash for all their basic needs. What's more, every single thing they consume has to be brought in from outside, increasing CO_2 emissions and placing a further burden on the environment. The major beneficiaries are the large transnational employers for whom the migrants represent a source of cheap and compliant labor.

Preventing further urbanization in the South requires programs that actively support the rural economy. In this regard, renewable energy technologies can play a vital role. Many parts of the South are blessed with abundant sunshine, which could be tapped for a range of both domestic and commercial uses. Other areas have wind, water or geothermal potential. Renewable energy technologies hold out the possibility of truly sustainable development. They are non-polluting and can be adapted to different cultural and ecological environments. They would cost a fraction of the sums of money currently being poured into huge dams, greenhouse gas-emitting, coal-fired plants and nuclear power.

Such changes cannot come about without a major shift of emphasis in the economies of the North. For decades, northern-based corporations have used the South as both larder and dumping ground—stripping whole countries of their natural resources. This process is now accelerating as corporations comb the globe for ever-cheaper resources and labor.

Clearly, the North needs to localize and that means producing vastly more of the goods it consumes closer to home so that no more of the best farm land in Kenya is turned over to growing cut flowers for the Netherlands, no more Brazilian rainforest is cut down to produce grain to feed the animals that will furnish Americans with hamburgers.

The consequences of allowing globalization to continue uncontrolled are hard to predict but would certainly include massive and irreversible damage to the Earth's climate. We have no choice but to promote a decentralized development model that would both strengthen local economies and reduce pollution. Neither the North nor the South can afford to wait. We all need to localize now.

VIEWPOINT

"Our protectionism may lead to greater problems in the future."

Protecting Local Economies from Globalization Is Harmful

Johan Norberg

According to Johan Norberg in the following viewpoint, policies that protect local economies are harmful to both poor and rich nations. Tariffs and other policies that block the import of food and products from developing nations into Europe and the United States, Norberg claims, deprive people in poor countries of billions of dollars in yearly export income. Protectionist policies also hurt developed nations such as the United States, Norberg argues, because they breed anti-West sentiment. Norberg is author of *In Defense of Global Capitalism.*

As you read, consider the following questions:

1. According to Norberg, what does Europe do with its surplus of foodstuffs?
2. In the author's opinion, what have Western politicians come to understand about high marginal taxes?
3. According to the author, what will happen if no real global reforms are implemented?

Johan Norberg, "We Need Sincere Free Trade," *The National Post*, September 10, 2003.

On my way back from a recent vacation, I passed by three big sugar mills. There is nothing strange with that—except for the fact that I spent the vacation in southern Sweden. That's about as far north as Alaska. Sweden has a very short summer, the soil is frozen for several months, and the cattle have to be indoors most of the time. Not your ideal place for agriculture, you would think.

The Costs of Protectionism

Yet Swedish farmers along with others in the European Union enjoy a comfortable lifestyle, at the expense of poor countries in Eastern Europe, Africa and Latin America. That's because of the EU's Common Agricultural Policy (CAP), which is designed to protect European farmers from competitors in the developing world and elsewhere. (And America plays a similar game.)

The CAP uses quotas and tariffs of several hundred per cent to effectively block the importation of foreign foodstuffs. The result is a huge surplus of foodstuffs piling up around Europe that must be either used or destroyed. So the EU dumps the stuff in poor countries with the help of export subsidies, further undermining the livelihood of competitors abroad.

The EU's protectionism isn't unique; most rich countries have similar systems. And the barriers to imports are especially cruel to developing countries. Western duties (i.e., taxes) on manufactured goods are 30% above the global average.

The tariffs are not uniform but rise in proportion to how processed the product is. Partially processed products face, on average, 20% higher tariffs than raw resources. Finished products face almost 50% higher tariffs. To put it simply, developing countries can export fruits, but not the jam they make from those fruits.

Western politicians have come to understand that high marginal taxes are bad for their economies; when will they realize the same goes for developing countries?

Losing Credibility

For a long time there have been calls for change, especially with the Cairns group [a coalition] of big agricultural exporters (such as Brazil, Argentina, and Canada) and the United States pressing for free trade reforms. The problem is that the United States is strikingly short on credibility when America slaps tariffs on foreign steel.[1] All that free trade rhetoric is not taken seriously. The EU's protectionism is the most destructive for developing countries, but U.S. protectionism is catching up quickly, which gives the EU an excuse not to change anything. With the U.S. Congress' passage of the latest multi-billion dollar protectionist farm bill, and the dumping of food aid in countries without food shortages, American agricultural policies look a lot like the CAP.

Moral Colonialism

Imposing limits to trade to promote moral or environmental concerns amounts to a kind of colonialism. Its principle is "might makes right," with the larger, richer, most powerful countries lording it over the not-so-rich and not-so-powerful ones.

The United States can impose trade sanctions against India if Indian fishermen are nasty to cute dolphins. But India cannot realistically bar trade with the United States if Americans are nasty to cows.

Tomas Larsson, Cato Institute, January 15, 2002.

According to the United Nations Conference on Trade and Development, EU protectionism deprives developing countries of nearly US$700-billion in export income a year. That's almost 14 times more than poor countries receive in foreign aid. EU protectionism is a continuing tragedy, causing unnecessary hunger and disease. The Cold War "iron curtain" between East and West has been replaced with a customs curtain between North and South.

EU protectionism takes a toll on Europeans, too. The rich countries' protectionism costs their citizens almost US$1-billion every day. At that rate, you could fly all the cows in the OECD [Organisation for Economic Co-Operation and Development], 60 million of them, around the world every year in business class. In addition, the cows could be given almost

1. On December 3, 2003, President George W. Bush repealed the tariff amid pressure from the European Union and World Trade Organization.

US$3,000 each in pocket money to spend in tax-free shops during their stopovers.

Our protectionism may lead to greater problems in the future. We in the West used to tell the developing countries about the benefits of the free market. And we promised wealth and progress would certainly come if they changed and adopted our ways. Many did, only to find our markets are closed to them. No wonder, then, that Western countries are seen as hypocrites, producing resentment and a fertile ground for anti-American and anti-liberal ideas in many regions at a time when the West needs friends more than ever.

The . . . American-European plan on agricultural trade [signed in 2003] contains a lot of nice phrases, but no commitments. With no prospect of real reforms at the WTO meeting . . . in Cancun, the poor countries will refuse to take part in a fake "development round." The multilateral trade system will face a collapse. American and European companies will face obstacles to their exports. Many developing countries will give up on globalization.

Now is the time for bold free trade initiatives—and sincerity. Perhaps America needs a presidential candidate like the one who in 2000, said, "I intend to work to end barriers and tariffs everywhere so that the entire world trades in freedom. It is the fearful who build walls. It is the confident who tear them down." That candidate was George W. Bush. Where did he go?

"The same trends that make offshoring possible are creating new opportunities —and new jobs—throughout the U.S. economy."

Outsourcing Benefits the U.S. Economy

Robert T. Parry

"Offshoring"—outsourcing to other countries—is a longtime U.S. business practice that creates new opportunities for American workers, argues Robert T. Parry in the following viewpoint. Outsourcing is when companies contract to have some of their functions performed by other businesses. Offshoring makes foreign economies stronger, Parry maintains, which in turn increases the demand for U.S. goods and services, and thus creates new jobs. Moreover, he claims, when businesses outsource goods and services, their productivity increases, and increased productivity results in new jobs being created elsewhere. Parry is former president and chief executive officer of the Federal Reserve Bank of San Francisco.

As you read, consider the following questions:

1. According to Parry, what is the basic argument in favor of free trade?
2. What example does the author use to support his argument that globalization helps increase U.S. productivity?
3. In the author's view, what are the hallmarks of a flexible economy?

As a monetary policymaker, my main concern is the health of the U.S. economy. Although the economy turned in a pretty sluggish performance for a long while after the 2001 recession, it has shown some real strength over the last few quarters in terms of output growth and productivity.

But along the way, the jobs market performance was surprisingly disappointing. . . . This certainly raised concerns—not only for those looking for work, but also for us at the Fed [short for U.S. Federal Reserve Bank, America's central bank] and for other policymakers around the country.

In the discussions about jobs, a lot of attention has focused on trade and terms such as "globalization," "outsourcing," and "offshoring." The concern, of course, is that a free-trade environment is letting good jobs drain from the U.S. economy and wind up in China, India, and other countries where workers command much lower salaries. In the extreme, some would like to see restraints on trade to protect those jobs and halt the globalization trend.

Whether globalization is a threat or an opportunity for the U.S. economy is a big question with serious ramifications. Though I won't be able to cover all the issues, I hope to add a little balance to the discussion. I'll focus on four questions. (1) Why are most economists in favor of free trade? (2) What exactly are "outsourcing" and "offshoring"? (3) Is globalization a threat or an opportunity for the U.S. economy? (4) What can policies do to help U.S. workers?

Why Are Most Economists in Favor of Free Trade?

Basically, the argument is that everyone benefits when countries specialize in the type of production at which they're relatively most efficient. Consider this analogy with the family: No family tries to make everything that it eats, wears, and enjoys. If it's cheaper to buy something or have someone else do something, that's what a family does. Then individual family members can concentrate on becoming good at their jobs in order to pay for what they buy.

A nation is no different. If it costs less to make certain products abroad than it does in the U.S., then it's difficult to argue that U.S. consumers and U.S. companies should pay more for those products from U.S. producers. Instead, it makes sense to purchase those products more cheaply from abroad, whether they're hard goods, like VCRs, or services, like call centers. Then we can devote our resources to producing and exporting those goods where we have a relative advantage. The result is a twofold benefit—greater efficiency and lower costs for U.S. firms and consumers.

What Are Outsourcing and Offshoring?

In its broadest sense, outsourcing is simply contracting out functions that had been done in-house, a longtime U.S. practice. When a car manufacturer in Michigan buys brake pads from an intermediate supplier in Ohio rather than produce them in-house, that's outsourcing. When a company replaces its cleaning and cafeteria workers with an outside contractor who does the same services more cheaply, that's outsourcing. When a company contracts out its payroll, accounting, and software operations, that's outsourcing. Clearly, outsourcing can result in job losses if the outside supplier is more efficient and uses fewer workers.

Offshoring has been referred to as the global cousin of outsourcing. Instead of turning to domestic providers, firms may decide to purchase a good or service from overseas providers because of lower costs. Offshoring, too, has a long history in U.S. manufacturing; for example, firms in Mexico supply seat covers and wiper blades to Detroit automakers. What appears to be new about offshoring is that it's affecting workers in the service sector who never expected to see foreign competition for their jobs—data managers, computer programmers, medical transcriptionists, and the like.

How much offshoring is going on? That's difficult to say. We don't have official statistics, and there are a lot of unsettled measurement issues. But a couple of estimates that have gotten some press . . . suggest that the U.S. lost 100,000–170,000 jobs to foreign workers between 2000 and 2003. Those numbers sound high until you put them in the context of all the job turnover that occurs every year in the U.S. Each year, some 15 million jobs are lost for all kinds of reasons—voluntary employment changes, layoffs, firings, and so on. And in a growing economy, every year even more jobs are created.

Is Globalization a Threat or an Opportunity?

The answer to this question will focus on three important issues that are sometimes neglected in the discussion. First, globalization means that economic activity flows in both directions; although we may lose jobs to foreign workers, we also may gain jobs and boost economic activity. For example, data suggest that, in terms of office work, the U.S. insources far more than it outsources; that is, just as U.S. firms use the services of foreigners, foreign firms make even greater use of the services of U.S. residents. "Office work" refers to the category of business, professional, and technical services that includes computer programming, telecommunications, legal services, banking, engineering, management consulting, call centers, data entry, and other private services. In 2003, we bought about $77 billion worth of those services from foreigners, but the value of the services we sold to foreigners was far higher, over $130 billion. . . .

Creating Opportunities and Growth

My second point is that open trade creates opportunities in the U.S by helping foreign economies become stronger. As incomes grow in other countries, so does their demand for goods and services, many of which those countries will not be able to produce—just as the U.S. does not. This rise in foreign demand for imports is an opportunity for U.S. firms to compete to provide those products. And it would be a shame to miss that opportunity because of trade barriers our policymakers erected. It would mean lost export sales and lost jobs in those sectors.

Finally, globalization can help increase productivity growth in the U.S. The example of offshoring's effect on the spread of IT [information technology] in the U.S. and, therefore, on our economic growth illustrates the point. According to one estimate, the globalized production of IT hardware—that is, the offshoring of computer-related manufacturing, such as Dell computer factories in China—reduced the prices of computer and telecommunications equipment by 10%–30%. These price declines boosted the spread of IT throughout the U.S. economy and raised both productivity and growth.

The Outsourcing Bogeyman

Should Americans be concerned about the economic effects of outsourcing? Not particularly. Most of the numbers thrown around are vague, overhyped estimates. What hard data exist suggest that gross job losses due to offshore outsourcing have been minimal when compared to the size of the entire U.S. economy. The outsourcing phenomenon has shown that globalization can affect white-collar professions, heretofore immune to foreign competition, in the same way that it has affected manufacturing jobs for years. . . . The creation of new jobs overseas will eventually lead to more jobs and higher incomes in the United States. Because the economy—and especially job growth—is sluggish . . . commentators are attempting to draw a connection between offshore outsourcing and high unemployment. But believing that offshore outsourcing causes unemployment is the economic equivalent of believing that the sun revolves around the earth: intuitively compelling but clearly wrong.

Daniel W. Drezner, *Foreign Affairs*, May/June 2004.

Offshoring offers the potential to lower the prices of IT software and services as well. This will promote the further spread of IT—and of new business processes that take advantage of cheap IT. It also will create jobs for U.S. workers to design and implement IT packages for a range of industries and companies. Although some jobs are at risk, the same trends that make offshoring possible are creating new opportunities—and new jobs—throughout the U.S. economy.

The Importance of Productivity

I've mentioned productivity several times so far, and I want to focus on it briefly, because I think it plays a significant role in the discussion about jobs in the U.S. Over the past two years, U.S. productivity in the nonfarm business sector has grown at a 4.8% annual rate. In the short term, this increased productivity has let businesses satisfy the demand for their output without having to hire new workers on net. So, it appears that this extraordinary surge of increased efficiency in our economy explains much more about the jobs situation than offshoring, outsourcing, or globalization does.

Although, clearly, productivity creates pain for workers who are displaced, most economists agree that higher productivity is a good thing for the economy. Why? Because, in the long run, higher productivity is the only way to create higher standards of living across the economy.

The American worker's ability to produce more goods and services per hour has been the key to the U.S. economy's surprising success throughout its history. Consider the manufacturing and agricultural sectors, where more output can now be produced with fewer workers. The same trend has occurred in services: the U.S. used to have lots of elevator operators, telephone operators, bank tellers, and gas station attendants, but now technological advances have taken over many of these jobs. Likewise, the Internet has taken over many routine tasks from travel agents, stock brokers, and accountants. And, with high-speed data links, a lot of office work can be done more cheaply abroad.

What happens to the displaced workers? They move into other sectors of the economy as new jobs emerge. For example, by one estimate, about a quarter of today's labor force is in jobs that didn't even exist in 1967.

This emergence of new jobs and workers' ability to move into them are the hallmarks of a flexible economy—that is, an economy in which labor and capital resources move freely among firms and industries. And such flexibility is a significant strength of the U.S. economy. We operate in competitive markets, and competition, whether from domestic or foreign competitors, induces change. To adapt to that change, and to ease the burden of adjusting to it, flexible labor and capital markets are critically important.

What Can Policies Do to Help U.S. Workers?

In terms of the overall economy, appropriate monetary and fiscal policies can ensure that aggregate demand keeps the economy on a sound footing, which helps generate jobs to replace those that have been lost.

But words about aggregate demand can seem like cold comfort to the individual workers whose offices and plants are closing because their jobs are going overseas. And concern for these workers, of course, is why there's interest in trying to restrict trade with tariffs, quotas, or other barriers. Indeed, such measures may actually succeed in slowing job losses in affected industries temporarily. But, as I hope I've illustrated, in the end, they impose significant costs on the rest of the economy that are much higher than any benefits.

That's why I believe it's far more appropriate to have policies that focus on protecting the people at risk, not the jobs. Such policies should aim to do two things during difficult transitions: help workers get through the hard times and help workers become more flexible so they can adapt when they do face these kinds of changes. In fact, we have policies like these—unemployment insurance, for example. We even have policies specifically for manufacturing workers who have lost jobs to foreign competition. These trade-adjustment assistance programs offer both financial support for a time and the opportunity for training, so that workers can retool their skills and find new jobs. So, in order to help the service workers who have lost their jobs because of outsourcing, it might be appropriate to extend these programs to them.

I realize there's some debate about how effective the programs are, but the concepts they're built on are, to my mind, right on target—giving workers a safety net and giving workers the training and tools to qualify for the jobs being created in the U.S. In fact, such programs also could be appropriate for workers who have lost jobs in the wake of the technology-driven productivity surge.

In the long-run, of course, the solution is simple to state, but difficult—and costly—to implement. And that solution is improving the performance of the U.S. education system. Education is the bedrock of our current edge in technology and productivity. It's the key to producing workers with the flexibility to learn new skills as market conditions evolve. And it's the hope and promise we must provide for future generations of Americans.

"The trickle of outsourcing threatens to become a flood."

Outsourcing Threatens American Workers

Tom Piatak

American workers have legitimate reasons to be concerned about the outsourcing of jobs to foreign countries, claims Tom Piatak in the following viewpoint. According to Piatak, as participation in global trade increases, more and more American jobs are at risk. In fact, he claims, America has not experienced job creation rates so low since the Great Depression, undoubtedly a result of outsourcing. Piatak is a contributing writer to *Chronicles*.

As you read, consider the following questions:

1. In Piatak's opinion, why is the popular outrage over outsourcing puzzling?
2. What types of jobs are students who were previously interested in engineering pursuing, in the author's view?
3. According to the author, why is education not the answer to jobs lost to outsourcing?

[In early 2004], Hewlett-Packard CEO Carly Fiorina defended her company's decision to send American jobs to Asia by declaring, "There is no job that is America's God-given right anymore." She probably did not mean to include CEOs of Fortune 500 corporations in this statement—Hyderabad [India] does not offer all the amenities she is used to, after all—but her blunt declaration that patriotism has no place in the board room perfectly captures the logic behind outsourcing.

Fiorina's sentiments were echoed by Greg Mankiw, the chairman of President [George W.] Bush's Council of Economic Advisors, who observed that "outsourcing is just a new way of doing international trade" that would help the U.S. economy "in the long run." President Bush's response to outsourcing has been to denounce the "economic isolationists" who would rather see high-paying computer jobs stay in the United States.

Americans Are Concerned

The majority of Americans, however, do not share the One Worldism of the Fortune 500 and the Bush administration. A recent Gallup Poll revealed that 61 percent of Americans are concerned that they or a friend or relative might lose a job to outsourcing. The same poll showed that 85 percent of Americans feel that a candidate's stand on outsourcing will be important in how they vote, with 58 percent saying that it will be "very important." It is safe to say that not many of these voters are as enthusiastic about their jobs disappearing as Carly Fiorina is.

In one sense, the popular outrage over outsourcing is a bit puzzling. As Mankiw noted, outsourcing is perfectly consistent with the free-trade ideology that has been embraced by the elites of both parties. Those elites, however, have been telling us that, even though the loss of manufacturing jobs was somehow "inevitable," we would prosper because high-paying computer and technical jobs would be ours. The rise of outsourcing has exposed this fatuousness, as corporations rush to replace their American technical employees with foreigners. The unemployment rate for electrical engineers stands at 6.2 percent, higher than the national average.

News stories have described how students previously interested in engineering are now pursuing jobs that they expect will continue to be performed here, such as those in law and the ever-growing government bureaucracy. And the trickle of outsourcing threatens to become a flood. Forrester Research projects that 500,000 computer-programming and information-technology jobs will migrate to India alone by 2015, joining a projected total of 3.3 million private-sector service jobs moving abroad over the same period. Predictions from the University of California-Berkeley run somewhat higher: 14 million American jobs could be outsourced in the next decade.

The Blunt Truth

Despite the platitudes mouthed by the Bush administration, the answer is not more education. After all, many of the jobs being sent overseas require great intelligence and an advanced education. It is not a lack of education that is causing American engineers to be replaced by Indian engineers making one fifth of what they do. Those jobs will continue to move overseas, at least until American engineers' salaries have dropped to the point where it is no longer attractive to replace them with Indians. In fact, the Bureau of Labor Statistics . . . released a list of the 19 fastest-growing occupations in America, and only two—registered nurses and post-secondary education—require any advanced education at all. The blunt truth is that we can expect any job that is open to foreign competition will be performed by declining numbers of Americans at wages facing continued downward pressure.

As shown by both the February and the March [2004] job figures, the growth areas in our free-trade economy are government and areas subsidized by government, such as education and health services (which together accounted for 36,000 of the 46,000 jobs added in February), and areas insulated from foreign competition, such as retail trade, leisure and hospitality, and construction (which, together with government-related employment, accounted for over 70 percent of the job growth in March). Although the more robust March job figures are good news, this remains the slowest recovery in terms of job creation since the 1930's. Reporter

Thompson. Copyright © 2003 by Copley News Service. Reproduced by permission.

John Allen, writing in the March 7, 2004, *Washington Post*, cites Georgetown economist Harry Holzer, who notes that there has not been a similar decline in payroll jobs since the 1930's, and Johns Hopkins economist Arnold Packer, who observes that employees' share of the value added to the U.S. economy has fallen to its lowest point since such records were first kept in 1947. Four million Americans have run through unemployment benefits without finding a job, and inflation-adjusted hourly wages have barely risen over the last year—even though the economy was growing during that entire time.

A Return to Economic Patriotism

More and more Americans are coming to believe that there may be something fundamentally wrong with our economy. And even some economists and businessmen are starting to rethink their adherence to free-trade ideology. CNN's Lou Dobbs has made opposition to outsourcing something of a personal crusade. Economist Jeff Madrick, writing in the March 18, 2004, *New York Times*, cites several economists who now believe that their profession has seriously underestimated the costs of job dislocation caused by free trade. And supply-side economist Paul Craig Roberts, a staunch opponent of big government and one of the architects of Ronald Reagan's 1981 tax cut, has written column after column exposing the fallacies of free-trade ideology.

The antidote to outsourcing is a return to economic patriotism by businessmen, consumers, and government. Despite what free-trade ideologues maintain, this is not synonymous with big government. Our current "recovery" has seen continued job growth in government, while private-sector jobs have disappeared, and it is hard to see government diminishing when disappearing jobs and declining wages create more government dependents, including two-income families relying on government to help with childcare and with the "advanced education" that is being touted as the remedy to job displacement. By contrast, before America embraced free trade, government was small, taxes were low, and families largely cared for themselves. Maybe that was not a coincidence.

7

VIEWPOINT

"The importance of international cooperation has come into sharp focus across the broad spectrum of global issues."

Nations Must Cooperate to Ensure That Globalization Benefits All

Eduardo Aninat

Making the benefits of globalization available to all countries requires international cooperation, claims Eduardo Aninat in the following viewpoint. Globalization provides the best hope for human welfare and world peace, he maintains, but all nations do not yet share its benefits. To make sure that globalization benefits rather than harms poor nations, concerted international action governed by open, cooperative global institutions is necessary, he insists. Aninat was deputy managing director of the International Monetary Fund from December 1999 to June 2003.

As you read, consider the following questions:

1. According to Aninat, what shift did the globalization debate undergo in 2001?
2. What do averages indicating that poverty declines with economic growth hide, in the author's opinion?
3. In the author's view, what are the four key challenges of globalization?

Eduardo Aninat, "Surmounting the Challenges of Globalization," *Finance & Development*, vol. 39, March 2002, pp. 4–7.

Globalization—the process through which an increasingly free flow of ideas, people, goods, services, and capital leads to the integration of economies and societies—has brought rising prosperity to the countries that have participated. It has boosted incomes and helped raise living standards in many parts of the world, partly by making sophisticated technologies available to less advanced countries. Since 1960, for example, life expectancy in India has risen by more than 20 years, and illiteracy in Korea has gone from nearly 30 percent to almost zero. These improvements are due to a number of factors, but it is unlikely that they could have occurred without globalization. In addition, greater integration has promoted human freedom by spreading information and increasing choices.

But in recent years, concerns have grown about the negative aspects of globalization and especially about whether the world's poorest—the 1.2 billion people who still live on less than $1 a day—will share in its benefits. The beliefs that free trade favors only rich countries and that volatile capital markets hurt developing countries the most have led activists of many stripes to come together in an "antiglobalization" movement. The activists highlight the costs of rapid economic change, the loss of local control over economic policies and developments, the disappearance of old industries, and the related erosion of communities. They also criticize international organizations for moving too slowly in tackling these concerns.

A New Approach

The year 2001, however, saw the debate undergo a subtle but perhaps profound shift, with both sides seeming to step back from approaching it in terms of whether globalization was "good" or "bad"—an approach that seemed overly simplistic. This recognition gained momentum in the wake of the September 11 [2001] terrorist attacks in the United States, which exposed the vulnerability of globalization that stems in part—but only in part—from the sense of hopelessness present in some countries unwilling or unable to embrace it.

Both sides increasingly realized that the debate should center on how best to manage the process of globalization—

at the national and international levels—so that the benefits are widely shared and the costs kept to a minimum. There is no question that greater integration into the world economy and more openness to other cultures offers all citizens of the global village a more hopeful future. Globalization, by offering a brighter future for all, provides perhaps the surest path to greater global security and world peace.

This understanding should attract support for the work needed to address the remaining challenges of globalization head-on. But there is an urgent need for a broad global debate on how these challenges can best be met and on who should play what role. This debate . . . will need to continue. The IMF [International Monetary Fund], along with the World Bank, has contributed significantly . . . by helping to focus . . . on global priorities, such as the Millennium Development Goals.[1] The IMF, focusing on its mandate and areas of expertise, is also continuing to readapt itself to better help countries meet the challenges of globalization.

Globalization Today

The world has experienced successive waves of what we now call globalization, going back as far as Marco Polo in the thirteenth century. These periods have all shared certain characteristics with our own: the expansion of trade, the diffusion of technology, extensive migration, and the cross-fertilization of diverse cultures—a mix that should give pause to those who perceive globalization narrowly, as a process nurtured strictly by economic forces.

By the end of the nineteenth century, the world was already highly globalized. Falling shipping costs had led to a rapid rise in trade, and in 1913 the ratio of world trade to world output reached a peak that would not be matched again until 1970. The growth of trade was accompanied by unprecedented flows of capital (as high as 10 percent of GDP, in net terms, in a number of both investor and recipient

1. The Millennium Development Goals are to eradicate extreme poverty and hunger; achieve universal primary education; promote gender equality and empower women; reduce child mortality; improve maternal health; combat HIV/AIDS, malaria, and other diseases; ensure environmental sustainability; and develop a global partnership for development.

countries) and migration (for many countries, ½ of 1 percent of population a year), especially to the Americas.

Following the two world wars and the Great Depression, a new wave of globalization began, characterized by further declines in transport costs, which fell by half in real terms from 1940 to 1960; the expansion of modern multinational corporations, which are well suited to working around barriers to trade imposed by language, national commercial policies, and other factors; and unprecedented growth in output and living standards.

The Impact of Technology

More recently, globalization has been reinvigorated by the unprecedented ease with which information can be exchanged and processed thanks to breakthroughs in computer and telecommunications technologies, which since 1970 have reduced real computing and communications costs by 99 percent. This technological progress has steadily expanded the range and quality of services that can be traded, including those that support trade in goods, moving us toward a globally integrated economy.

Is this a development to be welcomed? Economic theory suggests that a fully integrated world economy provides the greatest scope for maximizing human welfare. This proposition is based on assumptions about the free international movement of goods and factors of production (capital and labor), the availability of information, and a high degree of competition. But benefits accrue even if capital and labor cannot move freely, so long as goods are freely traded.

The Progress of Trade Liberalization

In the real world, we know that there are still many barriers to the free movement of capital and labor. And, indeed, important barriers to trade remain. There has, however, been substantial progress in trade liberalization since the Second World War. The . . . Doha Development Round of [international trade negotiations], for example, will be the tenth comprehensive trade round. Rising merchandise trade has been one of the hallmarks of the globalization process, and the gains from trade liberalization in recent decades have exceeded the costs by a very considerable margin. The Uruguay Round trade agreement reached in 1995 is estimated to have produced over $100 billion a year in net benefits, accruing mainly to those countries that have reduced trade barriers the most.

These trade gains have translated into faster economic growth and higher standards of living, as most clearly seen in East Asia: real incomes in Korea have doubled every 12 years since 1960. In the Spanish-speaking world, countries such as Spain, Mexico, and Chile have sharply boosted their shares of world trade and per capita incomes since 1980 by embracing globalization. A . . . World Bank study also suggests that the countries that have opened themselves to trade in the last two decades have, on average, grown the fastest. These "new globalizers" among developing countries have reduced import tariffs, on average, by 34 percentage points since 1980, compared with only 11 percentage points for those developing countries that, on average, saw no growth in per capita incomes over the period.

A Global Dialogue

To think globally—and to consider not only domestic factors, but also international ones as integral to decision-making today, in governments, businesses and organizations—does not mean a uniformity of thought, or just one approach. There are, quite naturally, a great variety of ways that we can think and act globally, and in so doing celebrate and strengthen global diversity.

In this sense, the local is not in opposition to the global, but is infused and enriched with global impulses and influences. Essential to realizing this new reality is a dialogue across nations and cultures based on common values and common concerns.

Kofi Annan, Yale University address, United Nations, October 2, 2002.

Moreover, we know that faster growth goes hand in hand with bigger declines in poverty and larger increases in life expectancy. A recent World Bank study by David Dollar and Aart Kraay takes this full circle by deducing that since, in broad terms, trade is good for growth, and growth is generally good for the poor—they find that, on average, increased growth raises the incomes of the poor in proportion to those of the population as a whole—then trade is good for the poor.

Capital market integration has also advanced substantially in recent decades. But while the benefits of trade globalization are relatively clear, developing countries need to have a set of preconditions in place to benefit from financial globalization and not to succumb to an increased probability of a currency or banking crisis occurring. That is why capital account liberalization is being approached with much greater caution than during the bullish years of the mid-1990s. Capital inflows contribute to growth by stimulating investment and technical progress and promoting efficient financial development. Openness to capital flows, when combined with sound domestic policies, gives countries access to a much larger pool of capital with which to finance development. Foreign direct investment in particular—as opposed to potentially volatile portfolio flows—speeds up both capital accumulation and the absorption of foreign technologies and, like trade, has been shown to promote economic growth.

A New Approach Post–September 11

Clearly, globalization has the potential to make all people better off. The problem is that there is no assurance that all people will be better off or that all changes will be positive. The studies that show that, on average, poverty declines with economic growth are encouraging. But averages hide the negative impact on individual countries and on certain groups within them. In addition, there are important questions about the relationships between economic policies and outcomes, especially the impact of macroeconomic and structural reform policies on poverty. For example, when is growth especially beneficial to the poor? And when does growth not benefit the poor? How does trade generate growth? Does all foreign capital raise growth? How can we best ensure that capital flows do no harm?

These are all questions on which the IMF is seeking a better understanding, and as we gain further insights, we will, if necessary, adjust our policy recommendations accordingly.

We are also committed to meeting four key challenges that fall in our areas of responsibility. The first is helping the poorest countries sustain the adjustment policies and structural reforms they need to reap the benefits of globalization. The second is increasing the stability of international financial markets—especially critical, given the importance of global financial stability as an international public good. The third is helping all of our members safely access these markets, including those countries that currently have no access. And the fourth is fostering a stable global macroeconomic environment. Only by addressing these challenges—in part through shared principles and rules—can we help our member countries accommodate the changes brought by globalization and cope with the dislocations such changes unavoidably bring.

But the atmosphere in which we are working has changed in some fundamental ways in the wake of the September 11 terrorist attacks—ways that provide an opportunity for a renewed dialogue. Even the antiglobalization movement that organized mass demonstrations in Seattle, Quebec, Genoa, and elsewhere has undergone profound change, as many of those who had been leading the protests against globalization—and against the IMF, the World Bank, and the World Trade Organization, in particular—are questioning whether such protests are an effective means to their ends. How have perceptions changed?

A Change in Perspectives

- It has become clear that the issues over which the debate has been conducted—issues central to the course of economic development—are governed by complex forces that defy glib generalization. It does not make sense to oppose globalization as such: the discussion must shift gears, aiming instead to identify effective ways to increase and spread the benefits of globalization while minimizing its costs.
- The importance of international cooperation has come into sharp focus across the broad spectrum of global issues. A by-product seems to be a renewed appreciation of the role of the Bretton Woods institutions [the World

Bank and the International Monetary Fund][2] as forums for global economic cooperation and of the role of the IMF in particular.

- It has become even clearer that, in the words of IMF Managing Director Horst Kohler, "there will not be a good future for the rich if there is no prospect of a better future for the poor." Besides being a moral question, poverty reduction is now recognized as a necessity for peace and security. The decision to launch the Doha talks is the first evidence that this recognition will translate into greater attention to the requirements of economic development.
- The weakening of world economic growth, manifest in early 2001 but exacerbated by the September 11 attacks, has revealed the fragility of global economic prosperity. The need for the kind of high-quality analysis that the IMF provides, helping to keep the global economy on an even keel, has become more evident.
- Some of the protesters seem to have decided to channel their energies less against the international organizations themselves and more toward their member governments. They see that pressing national governments to increase foreign aid and market access for exports from poor countries can result in far greater benefits for the poor than changes in the policies of international lending institutions.

Finding Solutions

So how should all parties proceed? First, besides finding solutions to problems, we need to find ways to implement them effectively. This means keeping in mind that issues formerly seen as national—including financial markets, the environment, labor standards, and economic accountability—are now seen to have international aspects. The ripple effects of actions taken in one country tend to be far greater and to travel faster than ever before. A purely national ap-

2. The Bretton Woods institutions are the World Bank and the International Monetary Fund. They were set up at a meeting of forty-three countries in Bretton Woods, New Hampshire, in July 1944. Their aims were to help rebuild the shattered postwar economy and to promote international economic cooperation.

proach to solving some problems risks merely pushing the problem across the frontier without providing a lasting solution even at the national level.

Second, we need to ensure that measures are taken to meet internationally agreed targets, such as the Millennium Development Goals, which include halving world poverty by 2015. Such measures would involve debt relief (especially for the heavily indebted poorest countries), social safety nets to cushion the short-term impact of economic reforms on the vulnerable, and higher social outlays, especially on health and education. In recent years, social outlays have been rising in countries with IMF-supported programs—significantly in countries benefiting from debt relief. Of course, this is only a modest beginning. For example, enormous additional resources are needed to improve health conditions in low-income and (for the poor) in middle-income countries, as pointed out in the World Health Organization's recent report of the Commission on Macroeconomics and Health.

Similarly, concerted action is needed to achieve the United Nations target that calls on rich countries to spend 0.7 percent of their GNP on development assistance. Action by the international community is also needed to open markets more broadly and effectively to exports from poor countries and to provide several of the poorest countries with lifesaving drugs at lower cost; the commitments made in Doha should serve as a minimum threshold for these goals.

Third, we need to revisit the institutions of global governance, to establish mechanisms to implement global solutions to global problems and to ensure that governments become more accountable. On economic issues, the importance countries attach to the open and cooperative multilateral system is reflected in the now virtually universal membership of the IMP [International Management Program] and the World Bank and the prospective accession of all major trading countries to the World Trade Organization. These three organizations address a very wide range of international economic issues, but they were not designed to be all-encompassing. Issues not central to any of their mandates are pressing and worthy of national and international attention. These include the environment, labor rights, international and local migration, and human rights, which must be addressed if globalization is to be sustained. As pointed out in the report by Michel Camdessus and others to the Bishops of the European Community, there are still many important institutional gaps in the present system.

Overall, this adds up to a weighty agenda for the international community, but perhaps never has so much been at stake, with so much potential within our reach. Globalization holds the promise of enormous benefits for the peoples of the world. To make this promise a reality, however, we must find a way to carefully manage the process. Better attention must be paid to reducing the negative effects and ensuring that the benefits are widely and fairly distributed. In this global village, we all need to work energetically toward that goal.

VIEWPOINT

"Proponents of international institutions should experiment with ways to improve accountability."

Global Institutions Must Be Made More Accountable

Joseph S. Nye Jr.

To increase their legitimacy, institutions of global governance such as the World Bank and the World Trade Organization must become more transparent and accountable, argues Joseph S. Nye Jr. in the following viewpoint. Global institutions can increase public access to their proceedings, he maintains, and experiment with new ways of selecting representatives. For example, nations could begin sending environmental ministers to World Trade Organization meetings to make sure environmentalists in each nation have a voice in formulating global policies. Nye, dean of Harvard University's Kennedy School of Government, is author with John D. Donahue of *Governance in a Globalizing World.*

As you read, consider the following questions:

1. In Nye's view, what concerns do protesters decrying globalization express?
2. According to the author, why are existing global institutions weak and hardly threatening?
3. How is accountability assured through means other than voting in well-functioning democracies, in the author's opinion?

Joseph S. Nye Jr., "Globalization's Democratic Deficit: How to Make International Institutions More Accountable," *Foreign Affairs,* July/August 2001. Copyright © 2001 by the Council on Foreign Relations, Inc. Reproduced by permission.

Seattle; Washington, D.C.; Prague; Quebec City [cities in which mass antiglobalization demonstrations were held]. It is becoming difficult for international economic organizations to meet without attracting crowds of protesters decrying globalization. These protesters are a diverse lot, coming mainly from rich countries, and their coalition has not always been internally consistent. They have included trade unionists worried about losing jobs and students who want to help the underdeveloped world gain them, environmentalists concerned about ecological degradation and anarchists who object to all forms of international regulation. Some protesters claim to represent poor countries but simultaneously defend agricultural protectionism in wealthy countries. Some reject corporate capitalism, whereas others accept the benefits of international markets but worry that globalization is destroying democracy.

Of all their complaints, this last concern is key. Protest organizers such as Lori Wallach attributed half the success of the Seattle coalition to "the notion that the democracy deficit in the global economy is neither necessary nor acceptable." For globalization's supporters, accordingly, finding some way to address its perceived democratic deficit should become a high priority.

It Is a Small World

Globalization, defined as networks of interdependence at worldwide distances, is not new. Nor is it just economic. Markets have spread and tied people together, but environmental, military, social, and political interdependence have also increased. If the current political backlash against globalization were to lead to a rash of protectionist policies, it might slow or even reverse the world's economic integration—as has happened at times in the past—even as global warming or the spread of the aids virus continued apace. It would be ironic if current protests curtailed the positive aspects of globalization while leaving the negative dimensions untouched.

Markets have unequal effects, and the inequality they produce can have powerful political consequences. But the cliche that markets always make the rich richer and the poor poorer is simply not true. Globalization, for example, has improved the lot of hundreds of millions of poor people around the world. Poverty can be reduced even when inequality increases. And in some cases inequality can even decrease. The economic gap between South Korea and industrialized countries, for example, has diminished in part because of global markets. No poor country, meanwhile, has ever become rich by isolating itself from global markets, although North Korea and Myanmar have impoverished themselves by doing so. Economic globalization, in short, may be a necessary, though not sufficient, condition for combating poverty.

The complexities of globalization have led to calls for a global institutional response. Although a hierarchical world government is neither feasible nor desirable, many forms of global governance and methods of managing common affairs already exist and can be expanded. Hundreds of organizations now regulate the global dimensions of trade, telecommunications, civil aviation, health, the environment, meteorology, and many other issues.

Antiglobalization protesters complain that international institutions are illegitimate because they are undemocratic. But the existing global institutions are quite weak and hardly threatening. Even the much-maligned World Trade Organization (WTO) has only a small budget and staff. Moreover, unlike self-appointed nongovernmental organizations (NGOs), international institutions tend to be highly responsive to national governments and can thus claim some real, if indirect, democratic legitimacy. International economic institutions, moreover, merely facilitate cooperation among member states and derive some authority from their efficacy.

Even so, in a world of transnational politics where democracy has become the touchstone of legitimacy, these arguments probably will not be enough to protect any but the most technical organizations from attack. International institutions may be weak, but their rules and resources can have powerful effects. The protesters, moreover, make some valid points. Not all member states of international organizations are themselves democratic. Long lines of delegation from multiple governments, combined with a lack of transparency, often weaken accountability. And although the organizations may be agents of states, they often represent only certain parts of those states. Thus trade ministers attend WTO meetings, finance ministers attend the meetings of the International Monetary Fund (IMF), and central bankers meet at the Bank for International Settlements in Basel. To outsiders, even within the same government, these institutions can look like closed and secretive clubs. Increasing the perceived legitimacy of international governance is therefore an important objective and requires three things: greater clarity about democracy, a richer understanding of accountability, and a willingness to experiment.

"We the People"

Democracy requires government by officials who are accountable and removable by the majority of people in a jurisdiction, together with protections for individual and minority rights. But who are "we the people" in a world where political identity at the global level is so weak? "One state, one vote" is not democratic. By that formula, a citizen of the Maldive Islands would have a thousand times more voting power than would a citizen of China. On the other hand, treating the world as a single global constituency in which the majority ruled would mean that the more than 2 billion Chinese and Indians could usually get their way. (Ironically, such a world would be a nightmare for those antiglobalization NGOs that seek international environmental and labor standards, since such measures draw little support from Indian or Chinese officials.)

In a democratic system, minorities acquiesce to the will of the majority when they feel they are generally full-fledged participants in the larger community. There is little evidence, however, that such a strong sense of community exists at the global level today, or that it could soon be created. In its absence, the extension of domestic voting procedures to the global level makes little practical or normative sense. A stronger European Parliament may reduce the "democratic deficit" within a union of relatively homogeneous European states, but it is doubtful that such an institution makes sense for the world at large. Alfred, Lord Tennyson's "Parliament of man" made for great Victorian poetry, but it does not stand up to contemporary political analysis. Democracy, moreover, exists today only in certain well-ordered nation-states, and that condition is likely to change only slowly.

Making Globalization Work

The most fundamental change that is required to make globalization work in the way that it should is a change in governance. Short of a fundamental change in governance, the most important way to ensure that international institutions are more responsive to the poor, to the environment, to . . . broader political and social concerns . . . is to increase openness and transparency.

Joseph Stiglitz, *TomPaine*, September 9, 2003.

Still, governments can do several things to respond to the concerns about a global democratic deficit. First, they can try to design international institutions that preserve as much space as possible for domestic political processes to operate. In the WTO, for example, the procedures for settling disputes can intrude on domestic sovereignty, but a country can reject a judgment if it pays carefully limited compensation to the trade partners injured by its actions. And if a country does defect from its WTO trade agreements, the settlement procedure limits the kind of tit-for-tat downward spiral of retaliation that so devastated the world economy in the 1930s. In a sense, the procedure is like having a fuse in the electrical system of a house: better the fuse blow than the house burn down. The danger with the WTO, therefore, is not that it prevents member states from accommodating domestic political choices but rather that members will be tempted to litigate too many disputes instead of resolving them through the more flexible route of political negotiations.

Creating Clearer Connections

Better accountability can and should start at home. If people believe that WTO meetings do not adequately account for environmental standards, they can press their governments to include environment ministers or officials in their WTO delegations. Legislatures can hold hearings before or after meetings, and legislators can themselves become national delegates to various organizations.

Governments should also make clear that democratic accountability can be quite indirect. Accountability is often assured through means other than voting, even in well-functioning democracies. In the United States, for example, the Supreme Court and the Federal Reserve Board respond to elections indirectly through a long chain of delegation, and judges and government bankers are kept accountable by professional norms and standards, as well. There is no reason that indirect accountability cannot be consistent with democracy, or that international institutions such as the IMF and the World Bank should be held to a higher standard than are domestic institutions.

Increased transparency is also essential. In addition to voting, people in democracies debate issues using a variety of means, from letters to polls to protests. Interest groups and a free press play important roles in creating transparency in domestic democratic politics and can do so at the international level as well. NGOs are self-selected, not democratically elected, but they too can play a positive role in increasing transparency. They deserve a voice, but not a vote. For them to fill this role, they need information from and dialogue with international institutions. In some instances, such as judicial procedures or market interventions, it is unrealistic to provide information in advance, but records and justifications of decisions can later be disclosed for comment and criticism—as the Federal Reserve and the Supreme Court do in domestic politics. The same standards of transparency should be applied to NGOs themselves, perhaps encouraged by other NGOs such as Transparency International.

The private sector can also contribute to accountability. Private associations and codes, such as those established by the international chemical industry in the aftermath of the Bhopal disaster,[1] can prevent a race to the bottom in standards. The practice of "naming and shaming" has helped consumers hold transnational firms accountable in the toy and apparel industries. And although people have unequal

1. In 1984 a gas leak at the Dow Chemical plant in Bhopal, India, killed thousands of people.

votes in markets, the aftermath of the Asian financial crisis may have led to more increases in transparency by corrupt governments than any formal agreements did. Open markets can help diminish the undemocratic power of local monopolies and reduce the power of entrenched and unresponsive government bureaucracies, particularly in countries where parliaments are weak. Moreover, efforts by investors to increase transparency and legal predictability can spill over to political institutions.

The New Democrats

Rather than merely rejecting the poorly formulated arguments of the protesters, proponents of international institutions should experiment with ways to improve accountability. Transparency is essential, and international organizations can provide more access to their deliberations, even if after the fact. NGOs could be welcomed as observers (as the World Bank has done) or allowed to file "friend of the court" briefs in WTO dispute-settlement cases. In some cases, such as the Internet Corporation for Assigned Names and Numbers (which is incorporated as a nonprofit institution under the laws of California), experiments with direct voting for board members may prove fruitful, although the danger of their being taken over by well-organized interest groups remains a problem. Hybrid network organizations that combine governmental, intergovernmental, and nongovernmental representatives, such as the World Commission on Dams or U.N. Secretary-General Kofi Annan's Global Compact, are other avenues to explore. Assemblies of parliamentarians can also be associated with some organizations to hold hearings and receive information, even if not to vote.

To the question of how to reconcile the necessary global institutions with democratic accountability. Highly technical organizations may be able to derive their legitimacy from their efficacy alone. But the more an institution deals with broad values, the more its democratic legitimacy becomes relevant. People concerned about democracy will need to think harder about norms and procedures for the governance of globalization. Neither denying the problem nor yielding to demagogues in the streets will do.

Periodical Bibliography

The following articles have been selected to supplement the diverse views presented in this chapter.

David A. Crocker	"Development Ethics and Globalization," *Philosophy & Public Policy Quarterly*, Fall 2002.
Pete Engardio, Aaron Bernstein, and Manjeet Kripalani	"Is Your Job Next?" *Business Week*, February 3, 2003.
Michael Eskew	"The 'I' in the Middle: Finding Common Ground in the Global Divide," *Vital Speeches of the Day*, June 1, 2002.
Fahed Fanek	"Globalization Needs Peace to Thrive," *Daily Star (Lebanon)*, January 2003.
Ann Florini	"Business and Global Governance: The Growing Role of Corporate Codes of Conduct," *Brookings Review*, Spring 2003.
Thomas Grennes	"Creative Destruction and Globalization," *CATO Journal*, Winter 2003.
Justin Heet	"America and the Coming Global Workforce," *American Outlook*, Winter 2004.
Bob Herbert	"Jobs Don't Vanish, They Go Abroad," *Liberal Opinion*, February 9, 2004.
Kenneth Himes	"Globalization's Next Phase," *Origins*, May 23, 2002.
Ernest F. Hollings	"Protectionism? In Fact, It Happens to Be Congress's Job," *Washington Post*, March 29–April 4, 2004.
William F. Jasper	"Losing America's Livelihood," *New American*, January 26, 2004.
Frank LaGrotta	"'Outsourcing' Our Lives," *Nation*, March 8, 2004.
David Lapin	"Globalization Brings Ethical Challenges," *IndUS Business Journal*, August 1, 2004.
James H. Mittelman	"Making Globalization Work for the Have Nots," *International Journal on World Peace*, June 2002.
J. Orstrom Moller	"Wanted: A New Strategy for Globalization," *Futurist*, January/February 2004.
Kevin Watkins	"Making Globalization Work for the Poor," *Finance & Development*, March 2002.

For Further Discussion

Chapter 1

1. While Abbas J. Ali sees globalization as a beneficial force, Cynthia Moe-Lobeda sees it as a destructive one. Both authors acknowledge that the way globalization is defined influences how it is perceived. Locate within the viewpoints how each author defines globalization. How does each author's definition of globalization color his or her perception of it?
2. Philippe Legrain sees globalization as the freedom to choose among a great variety of cultural forms. Maude Barlow, on the other hand, sees globalization as limiting cultural choices. Both cite examples to support their claim. Citing the viewpoints, which evidence do you find more convincing?
3. Daniel T. Griswold emphasizes the correlation between globalization and democracy and minimizes the importance of outliers, nations that do not fit the trend. Catharin E. Dalpino acknowledges the same correlation but places greater weight on the outliers in making her claim that the correlation does not support a causal relationship. Which analysis of the outliers do you find more persuasive? Explain.

Chapter 2

1. Steven Staples argues that globalization leads to war. Gerald P. O'Driscoll and Sara J. Cooper claim that countries that participate in global trade are less likely to wage war on each other. To support their arguments, the authors cite evidence of a correlation between globalization and war. One viewpoint cites a positive relationship, the other a negative one. Citing from the viewpoints, which evidence do you think is more persuasive?
2. Jerry Mander believes that unrestrained global corporations will harm the environment while John A. Charles argues that free trade benefits the environment. What evidence does each author offer to support his argument? Does the type of evidence each provides make one argument more or less persuasive? Explain, citing from the viewpoints.

Chapter 3

1. Brett D. Schaefer and Jim Peron both argue that globalization helps the poor in developing nations. Lila Rajiva and Antonia Juhasz concede that globalization has the potential to help the world's poor but as practiced is not doing so. All authors cite evidence to support their viewpoints, but each cites a different type of evidence. While some cite statistics, for example, others

cite personal observations. What type of evidence does each author cite, and which type do you find most persuasive? Why?

2. Soren Ambrose argues that relieving developing nations of oppressive global debts will help the world's poor. The International Monetary Fund and World Bank argue that canceling all debts will threaten the ability of international financial institutions to offer assistance to developing nations. How are the authors' institutional affiliations reflected in their viewpoints? Does this influence which argument you find more persuasive? Explain.
3. David Moberg opposes forcing developing nations to privatize public services in order to obtain development assistance. Amy Kapczynski opposes imposing international patent laws that make it difficult for the poor in developing nations to receive necessary medicines. Citing from the viewpoints, point out what assumptions about the motives of institutions of globalization—international lending institutions and multinational corporations—these authors share. Are these assumptions necessary for their arguments to be persuasive?

Chapter 4

1. Robert Reich contends that the Bush administration's trade policies are isolationist, thus preventing U.S. participation in globalization, while Jennifer A. Gritt argues that the administration's trade policies are internationalist, thus fostering U.S. participation in globalization. Citing from the viewpoints, which of these conflicting arguments do you find more persuasive? Or, is it possible that both arguments are valid? Explain.
2. Helena Norberg-Hodge argues that trade policies that promote local production and consumption will better serve the poor in developing nations. Johan Norberg sees localization as protectionism and a threat to the poor in developing nations. How does the way each author sees the people in the developing world color his or her attitude toward which global polices are best?
3. While Robert T. Parry sees outsourcing as a benefit to the U.S. economy and thus in the long run a benefit to American workers, Tom Piatak sees it as a threat. Piatak contends that Americans distrust claims of long-term benefits because U.S. economic experts have made false promises before. Citing evidence from the viewpoints, do you think distrust is warranted?
4. Eduardo Aninat and Joseph S. Nye Jr. suggest ways in which the institutions of globalization can be improved so that all who participate can benefit from it. What barriers to success does each author cite in his viewpoint?

Organizations to Contact

The editors have compiled the following list of organizations concerned with the issues debated in this book. The descriptions are derived from materials provided by the organizations. All have publications or information available for interested readers. The list was compiled on the date of publication of the present volume; names, addresses, phone and fax numbers, and e-mail and Internet addresses may change. Be aware that many organizations take several weeks or longer to respond to inquiries, so allow as much time as possible.

Bretton Woods Committee (BWC)
1990 M St. NW, Suite 450, Washington, DC 20036
(202) 331-1616 • fax: (202) 785-9423
e-mail: info@brettonwoods.org
Web site: www.brettonwoods.org

BWC is a bipartisan group dedicated to increasing public understanding of international financial and development issues and the role of the World Bank, International Monetary Fund, and World Trade Organization. Members include industry and financial leaders, economists, university leaders, and former government officials. On its Web site, BWC publishes the quarterly *BWC Newsletter* and reports, including *The United States and the WTO: Benefits of the Multilateral Trade System.*

Cato Institute
1000 Massachusetts Ave. NW, Washington, DC 20001-5403
(202) 842-0200 • fax: (202) 842-3490
e-mail: cato@cato.org • Web site: www.cato.org

The institute is a nonpartisan public policy research foundation dedicated to limiting the role of government and protecting individual liberties. It publishes the quarterly magazine *Regulation*, the bimonthly *Cato Policy Report*, and numerous policy papers and articles. Articles on globalization include "The Blessings and Challenges of Globalization," "Why Globalization Works," and "Globalization Serves the World's Poor," which are available on its Web site.

Competitive Enterprise Institute (CEI)
1001 Connecticut Ave. NW, Suite 1250, Washington, DC 20036
(202) 331-1010 • fax: (202) 331-0640
e-mail: info@cei.org • Web site: www.cei.org

CEI is a nonprofit public policy organization dedicated to advancing the principles of free enterprise and limited government. It believes that individuals are best helped not by government intervention, but by making their own choices in a free marketplace. CEI's publications include the monthly newsletter *Monthly Planet* and articles, including "The Winds Of Global Change: Which Way Are They Blowing?" and "The Triumph Of Democratic Capitalism: The Threat of Global Governance," which are available on its Web site.

Earth Island Institute
300 Broadway, Suite 28, San Francisco, CA 94133
(415) 788-3666 • fax: (415) 788-7324
e-mail: earthisland@earthisland.org
Web site: www.earthisland.org

Earth Island Institute's work addresses environmental issues and their relation to such concerns as human rights and economic development in the third world. The Institute's publications include the quarterly *Earth Island Journal.* The articles "Bucking the Corporate Future" and "In Favor of a New Protectionism" are available on its Web site.

50 Years Is Enough Network
3628 Twelfth St. NE, Washington, DC 20017
(202) 463-2265
Web site: www.50years.org

Founded on the fiftieth anniversary of the World Bank and International Monetary Fund, this coalitions of more than two hundred antiglobalization groups is dedicated to reforming the policies and practices of the two international financial institutions. On its Web site the network provides fact sheets and international debt-relief articles, including the fact sheets "Africa Needs Debt Cancellation, Not More IMF Programs" and "IMF/WB Debt Plan: Still Failing After All These Years."

Global Exchange
2017 Mission St., Suite 303, San Francisco, CA 94110
(415) 255-7296 • fax: (415) 255-7498
Web site: www.globalexchange.org

Founded in 1988, this nonprofit research, education, and action center seeks to link people in the Northern Hemisphere (first world) and Southern Hemisphere (third world) who are promoting social justice and democratic development. Global Exchange promotes a U.S. foreign policy that is noninterventionist. It publishes *Global Exchanges* quarterly.

Global Policy Forum (GPF)
777 UN Plaza, Suite 7G, New York, NY 10017
(212) 557-3161 • fax: (212) 557-3165
e-mail: globalpolicy@globalpolicy.org
Web site: www.globalpolicy.org

Global Policy Forum monitors policy making at the United Nations, promotes accountability of global decisions, educates and mobilizes citizen participation, and advocates on vital issues of international peace and justice. The forum publishes policy papers and the *GPF Newsletter*. On its Web site GPF provides an internal globalization link with subcategories on the topic, including politics, culture, and economics. The Web site provides charts, graphs, and articles, including "Measuring Globalization: Who's Up, Who's Down?"

Global Trade Watch (GTW)
215 Pennsylvania Ave. SE, Washington, DC 20003
(202) 546-4996
Web site: www.tradewatch.org

GTW promotes democracy by challenging corporate globalization, arguing that the current globalization model is neither a random inevitability nor "free trade." GTW works on an array of globalization issues, including health and safety, environmental protection, economic justice, and democratic and accountable governance. GTW publishes the book *Whose Trade Organization? A Comprehensive Guide to the WTO*. Fact sheets and articles, such as "Our World Is Not for Sale," are available on its Web site.

Heritage Foundation
214 Massachusetts Ave. NE, Washington, DC 20002
(202) 546-4400 • fax: (202) 546-0904
e-mail: info@heritage.org • Web site: www.heritage.org

The Heritage Foundation is a conservative think tank that supports the principles of free enterprise and limited government. Its many publications include the quarterly magazine *Policy Review* and the occasional-papers series Heritage Talking Points. On its Web site, the foundation includes articles on globalization such as "Why America Needs to Support Free Trade" and "Emerging Global Menace?"

Institute for International Economics (IIE)
1750 Massachusetts Ave. NW, Washington, DC 20036
(202) 328-9000 • fax: 202-659-3225
Web site: www.iie.com

A proglobalization research institution devoted to the study of global macroeconomic issues, investment, and trade, IIE has contributed to the development of the World Trade Organization and the North American Free Trade Agreement and other initiatives. The Institute publishes policy papers and books on globalization including *Trade Policy and Global Poverty.* Some speeches and articles are available on its Web site, including "Globalization and the International Financial System."

International Forum on Globalization (IFG)
1009 General Kennedy Ave., Suite 2, San Francisco, CA 94129
(415) 561-7650 • fax: (415) 561-7651
e-mail: ifg@ifg.org • Web site: www.ifg.org

IFG is a coalition of nongovernmental organizations that educates activists, policy makers, and the media about the effects of economic globalization. It publishes several books and reports on globalization, including *Intrinsic Consequences of Economic Globalization on the Environment* and *Alternatives to Economic Globalization.*

International Monetary Fund (IMF)
700 Nineteenth St. NW, Washington, D.C. 20431
(202) 623-7000 • fax: (202) 623-4661
e-mail: publicaffairs@imf.org • Web site: www.imf.org

The IMF is an international organization of 184 member countries. It was established to promote international monetary cooperation, exchange stability, and orderly exchange arrangements. IMF seeks to foster economic growth and high levels of employment and provides temporary financial assistance to countries. It publishes the quarterly *Finance & Development* as well as reports on its activities, including the quarterly *Global Financial Stability Report*, recent issues of which are available on its Web site along with data on IMF finances and individual country reports.

Ruckus Society
4131 Shafter Ave., Suite 9, Oakland, CA 94609
(510) 595-3442 • fax: (510) 763-7068
e-mail: info@ruckus.org • Web site: www.ruckus.org

The organization teaches nonviolent, civil disobedience skills to environmental and human rights organizations and helps other groups carry out "direct-action" protests. On its Web site, Ruckus publishes news articles on its activities from media supporters and opponents. The society publishes training manuals for nonviolent direct action, which are available on its Web site.

United Nations Development Programme (UNDP)
1 United Nations Plaza, New York, NY 10017
(212) 906-5315 • fax: (212) 906-5364
Web site: www.undp.org

UNDP funds six thousand projects in more than 150 developing countries and territories. It works with governments, UN agencies, and nongovernmental organizations to enhance self-reliance and promote sustainable human development. Its priorities include improving living standards, protecting the environment, and applying technology to meet human needs. UNDP's publications include the weekly newsletter *UNDPFlash*, the human development magazine *Choices*, and the annual *UNDP Human Development Report*. On its Web site, UNDP publishes the *Millennium Development Goals*, its annual report, regional data and analysis, speeches and statements, and recent issues of its publications.

World Bank
1818 H St. NW, Washington, DC 20433
(202) 477-1234 • fax: (202) 577-0565
Web site: www.worldbank.org

Formally known as the International Bank for Reconstruction and Development, the World Bank seeks to reduce poverty and improve the standard of living of poor people around the world. It promotes sustainable growth and investments in developing countries through loans, technical assistance, and policy guidance. The World Bank publishes books on global issues, including *Global Economic Prospects 2005: Trade, Regionalism, and Development*; *Privatization in Latin America: Myths and Reality*; and *Intellectual Property and Development: Lessons from Recent Economic Research*. On its Web site, the World Bank provides current development data and programs.

World Trade Organization (WTO)
Centre William Rappard, Rue de Lausanne 154, CH-1211
Geneva 21, Switzerland
(41-22) 739 51 11 • fax: (41-22) 731 42 06
e-mail: enquiries@wto.org • Web site: www.wto.org

WTO is a global international organization that establishes rules dealing with the trade between nations. Two WTO agreements have been negotiated and signed by the bulk of the world's trading nations and ratified in their parliaments. The goal of these agreements is to help producers of goods and services, exporters, and importers conduct their business. WTO publishes trade statistics, research and analysis, studies, reports, and the journal *World Trade Review*. Recent publications are available on the WTO Web site.

Worldwatch Institute

1776 Massachusetts Ave. NW, Washington, DC 20036-1904
(202) 452-1999 • fax: (202) 296-7365
e-mail: worldwatch@worldwatch.org
Web site: www.worldwatch.org

Worldwatch is a research organization that analyzes and calls attention to global problems, including environmental concerns such as the loss of cropland, forests, habitat, species, and water supplies. It compiles the annual *State of the World* anthology and publishes the bimonthly magazine *World Watch* and the World Watch Paper Series, which includes "Home Grown: The Case or Local Food in a Global Market" and "Underfed and Overfed: The Global Epidemic of Malnutrition."

Bibliography of Books

Robert E. Baldwin and L. Alan Winters, eds. *Challenges to Globalization: Analyzing the Economics*. Chicago: University of Chicago Press, 2004.

Loudes Beneria and Savitri Bisnath, eds. *Global Tensions: Challenges and Opportunities in the World Economy*. New York: Routledge, 2004.

Jagdish N. Bhagwati *In Defense of Globalization*. New York: Oxford University Press, 2004.

Paul Blustein *The Chastening: Inside the Crisis that Rocked the Global Financial System and Humbled the IMF.* New York: Public Affairs, 2001.

Jeremy Brecher, Tim Costello, and Brendan Smith *Globalization from Below: The Power of Solidarity*. Cambridge, MA: South End Press, 2000.

Alan Bryman *The Disneyization of Society*. Thousand Oaks, CA: Sage, 2004.

Zbigniew Brzezinski *The Choice: Global Domination or Global Leadership*. New York: Basic Books, 2004.

Fritjof Capra *The Hidden Connections: A Science for Sustainable Living*. New York: Doubleday, 2002.

John Cavanagh and Jerry Mander, eds. *Alternatives To Economic Globalization: A Better World Is Possible*. San Francisco: Berrett-Koehler, 2004.

Amy Chua *World on Fire: How Exporting Free Market Democracy Breeds Ethnic Hatred and Global Instability*. New York: Doubleday, 2003.

Dilip K. Das *Financial Globalization and the Emerging Market Economics*. New York: Routledge, 2004.

John Eatwell and Lance Taylor *Global Finance at Risk: The Case for International Regulation*. New York: New Press, 2000.

Jonathan Friedman and Shalini Randeria, eds. *Worlds on the Move: Globalization, Migration, and Cultural Security*. New York: Palgrave Macmillan, 2004.

Anthony Giddens *Runaway World: How Globalization Is Reshaping Our Lives*. New York: Routledge, 2000.

Kent Albert Jones *Who's Afraid of the WTO?* New York: Oxford University Press, 2004.

Roger King *The State, Democracy, and Globalization*. New York: Palgrave Macmillan, 2004.

Brink Lindsey *Against the Dead Hand: The Uncertain Struggle for Global Capitalism*. New York: John Wiley & Sons, 2002.

Ronnie D. Lipschutz	*Global Environmental Politics: Power, Perspectives, and Practice.* Washington, DC: CQ Press, 2004.
Edward D. Mansfield, ed.	*International Conflict and the Global Economy.* Northhampton, MA: Edward Elgar Pub, 2004.
Tom Mertes, ed.	*A Movement of Movements: Is Another World Really Possible?* New York: Verso, 2004.
William M. Mott	*Globalization: People, Perspectives, and Progress.* Westport, CT: Praeger, 2004.
Johan Norberg	*In Defense of Global Capitalism.* Washington, DC: Cato Institute, 2003.
Patrick O'Meara, Howard D. Mehlinger, and Matthew Krain, eds.	*Globalization and the Challenges of the New Century.* Bloomington: Indiana University Press, 2000.
Diane Perrons	*Globalization and Social Change: People and Places in a Divided World.* New York: Routledge, 2004.
Jan Nederveen Pieterse	*Globalization and Culture: Global Mélange.* Lanham, MD: Rowman & Littlefield, 2004.
Harry Redner	*Conserving Cultures: Technology, Globalization, and the Future of Local Cultures.* Lanham, MD: Rowman & Littlefield, 2004.
Donald M. Snow	*National Security for a New Era: Globalization and Geopolitics.* New York: Pearson/Longman, 2004.
George Soros	*On Globalization.* New York: Public Affairs, 2004.
James Gustave Speth	*Red Sky at Morning: America and the Crisis of the Global Environment.* New Haven, CT: Yale University Press, 2004.
James Gustave Speth	*Worlds Apart: Globalization and the Environment.* Washington, DC: Island Press, 2003.
Amory Starr	*Naming the Enemy: Anti-Corporate Movements Confront Globalization.* London: Zed Books, 2001.
Manfred B. Steger, ed.	*Rethinking Globalism.* Lanham, MD: Rowman & Littlefield, 2004.
Joseph E. Stiglitz	*Globalization and its Discontents.* New York: W.W. Norton, 2002.
Ian Vasquez	*Global Fortune: The Stumble and Rise of World Capitalism.* Washington, DC: Cato Institute, 2000.

Index